My Life Beyond
ASTHMA

A Mayo Clinic patient story
by Hey Gee and Charles

MAYO CLINIC PRESS KIDS

This book is a collaboration between
Fondation Ipsen and Mayo Clinic.

The story has been inspired by
Charles' experience with asthma.

The words in bold refer to key terms on page 32.

MEDICAL EDITOR

Manuel Arteta, M.D., Consultant, Division of Pediatric Pulmonology,
Mayo Clinic, Rochester, MN; Assistant Professor of Pediatrics,
Mayo Clinic College of Medicine and Science

SERIES CONCEPTION

Fredric B. Meyer, M.D., Consultant, Department of Neurologic Surgery,
Mayo Clinic, Rochester, MN; Executive Dean of Education,
Professor of Neurosurgery, Mayo Clinic College of Medicine and Science

James A. Levine, M.D., Ph.D., Professor, President, Fondation Ipsen, Paris, France

Foreword

Hi!

My name is Charles. I am 8 years old, and I have asthma. Sometimes when I get a cold, when I run around outside in the cold and when I'm around smoke, I have trouble breathing, and I cough a lot. I also have trouble when the air quality is bad, like from recent wildfires. The coughing can make it difficult to concentrate in school or take part in activities.

Just like in this book, I love to go on all types of adventures. My inhaler really helps so I can do these activities just like other kids. I don't let asthma stop me from anything I want to do or any adventure I want to go on. I hope reading this book will inspire you to do the same.

"

WITH YOUR ASTHMA UNDER CONTROL, YOU CAN TAKE ON ANY ADVENTURE

"

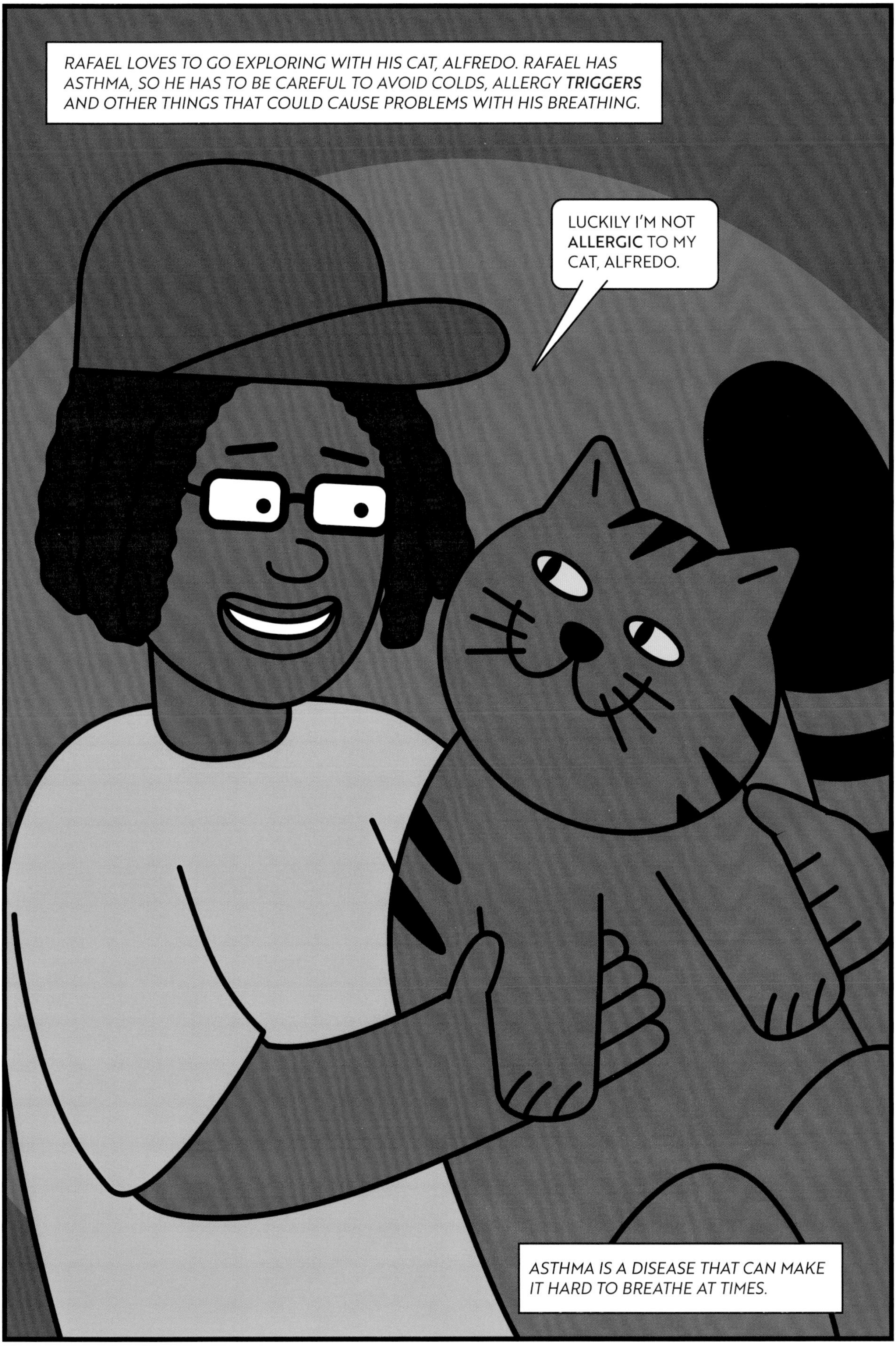
RAFAEL LOVES TO GO EXPLORING WITH HIS CAT, ALFREDO. RAFAEL HAS ASTHMA, SO HE HAS TO BE CAREFUL TO AVOID COLDS, ALLERGY **TRIGGERS** AND OTHER THINGS THAT COULD CAUSE PROBLEMS WITH HIS BREATHING.
LUCKILY I'M NOT **ALLERGIC** TO MY CAT, ALFREDO.
ASTHMA IS A DISEASE THAT CAN MAKE IT HARD TO BREATHE AT TIMES.

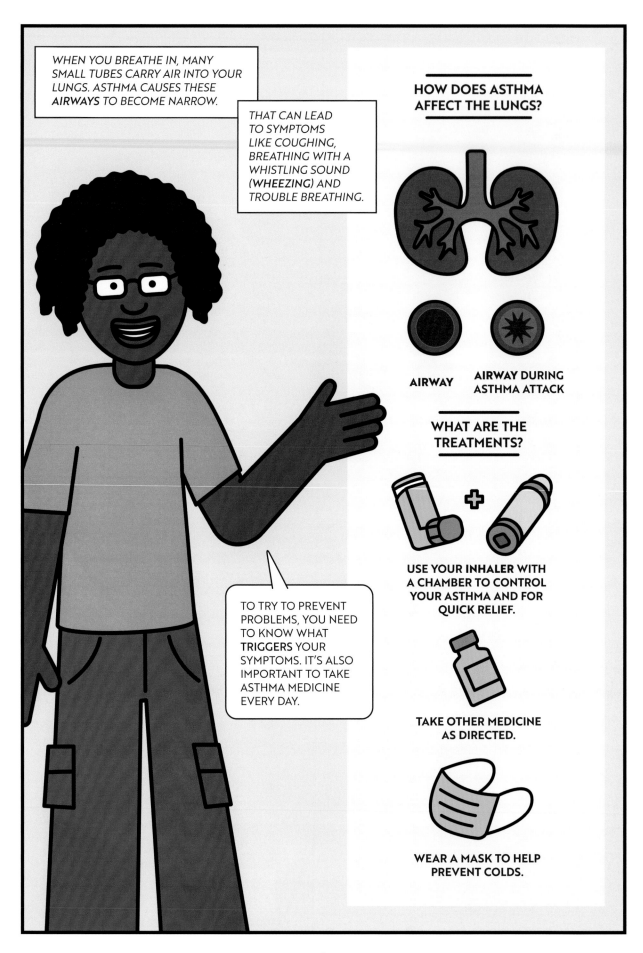

WHEN YOU BREATHE IN, MANY SMALL TUBES CARRY AIR INTO YOUR LUNGS. ASTHMA CAUSES THESE **AIRWAYS** TO BECOME NARROW.

THAT CAN LEAD TO SYMPTOMS LIKE COUGHING, BREATHING WITH A WHISTLING SOUND (**WHEEZING**) AND TROUBLE BREATHING.

TO TRY TO PREVENT PROBLEMS, YOU NEED TO KNOW WHAT **TRIGGERS** YOUR SYMPTOMS. IT'S ALSO IMPORTANT TO TAKE ASTHMA MEDICINE EVERY DAY.

HOW DOES ASTHMA AFFECT THE LUNGS?

AIRWAY

AIRWAY DURING ASTHMA ATTACK

WHAT ARE THE TREATMENTS?

USE YOUR **INHALER** WITH A CHAMBER TO CONTROL YOUR ASTHMA AND FOR QUICK RELIEF.

TAKE OTHER MEDICINE AS DIRECTED.

WEAR A MASK TO HELP PREVENT COLDS.

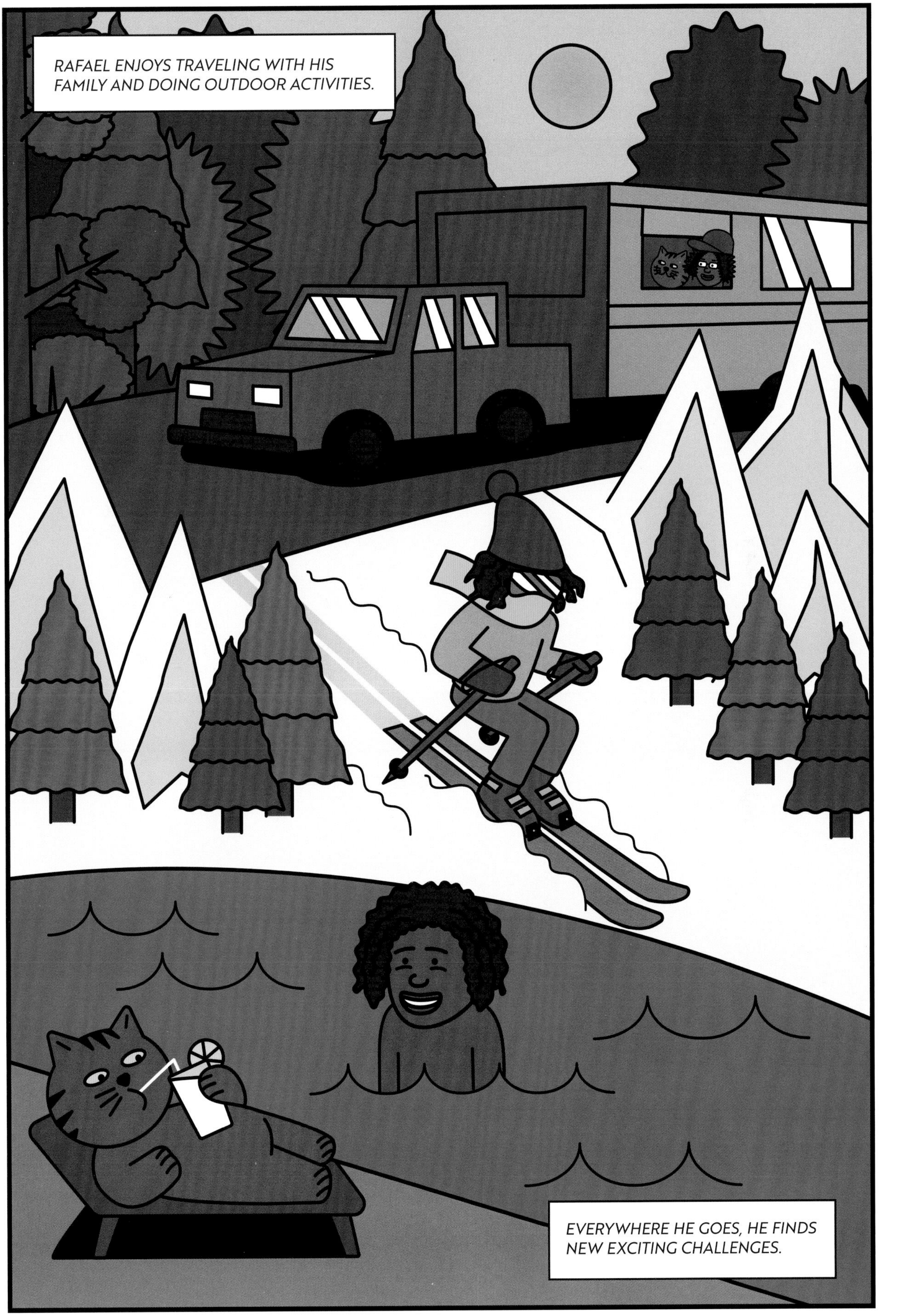
RAFAEL ENJOYS TRAVELING WITH HIS FAMILY AND DOING OUTDOOR ACTIVITIES.
EVERYWHERE HE GOES, HE FINDS NEW EXCITING CHALLENGES.

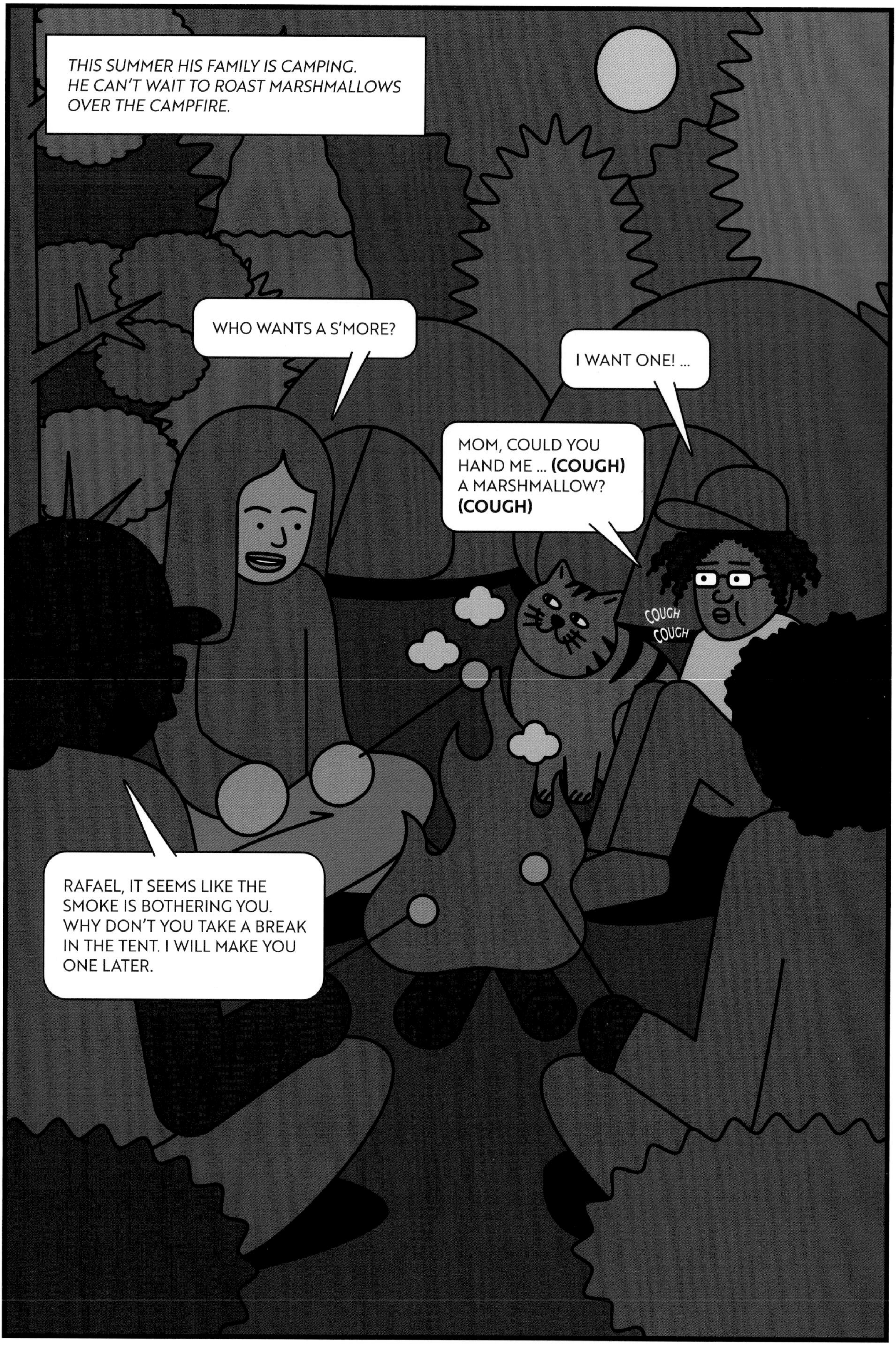

THIS SUMMER HIS FAMILY IS CAMPING. HE CAN'T WAIT TO ROAST MARSHMALLOWS OVER THE CAMPFIRE.
WHO WANTS A S'MORE?
I WANT ONE! ...
MOM, COULD YOU HAND ME ... **(COUGH)** A MARSHMALLOW? **(COUGH)**
COUGH COUGH
RAFAEL, IT SEEMS LIKE THE SMOKE IS BOTHERING YOU. WHY DON'T YOU TAKE A BREAK IN THE TENT. I WILL MAKE YOU ONE LATER.

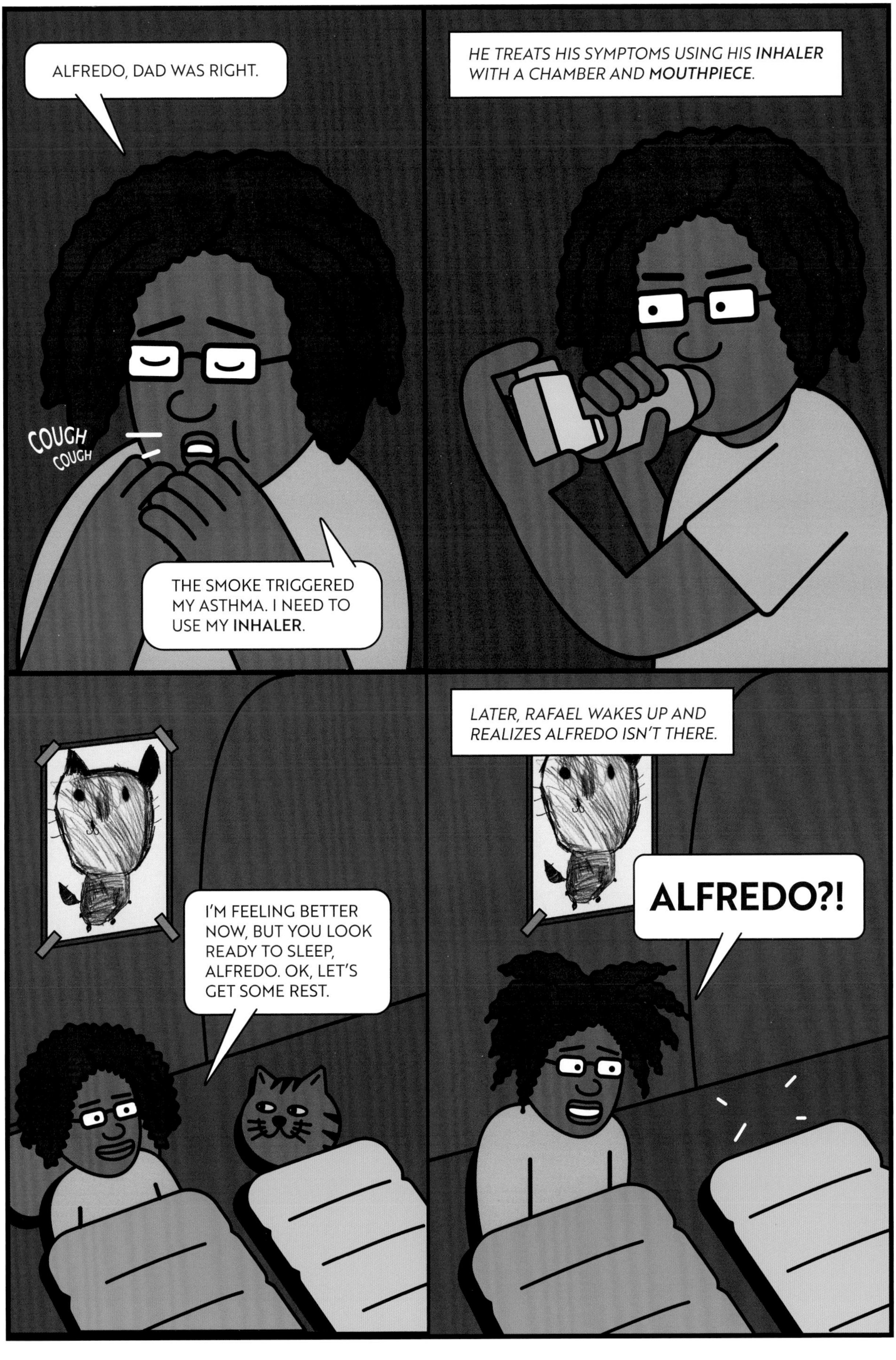
ALFREDO, DAD WAS RIGHT.
COUGH COUGH
THE SMOKE TRIGGERED MY ASTHMA. I NEED TO USE MY **INHALER**.
*HE TREATS HIS SYMPTOMS USING HIS **INHALER** WITH A CHAMBER AND **MOUTHPIECE**.*
I'M FEELING BETTER NOW, BUT YOU LOOK READY TO SLEEP, ALFREDO. OK, LET'S GET SOME REST.
LATER, RAFAEL WAKES UP AND REALIZES ALFREDO ISN'T THERE.
ALFREDO?!

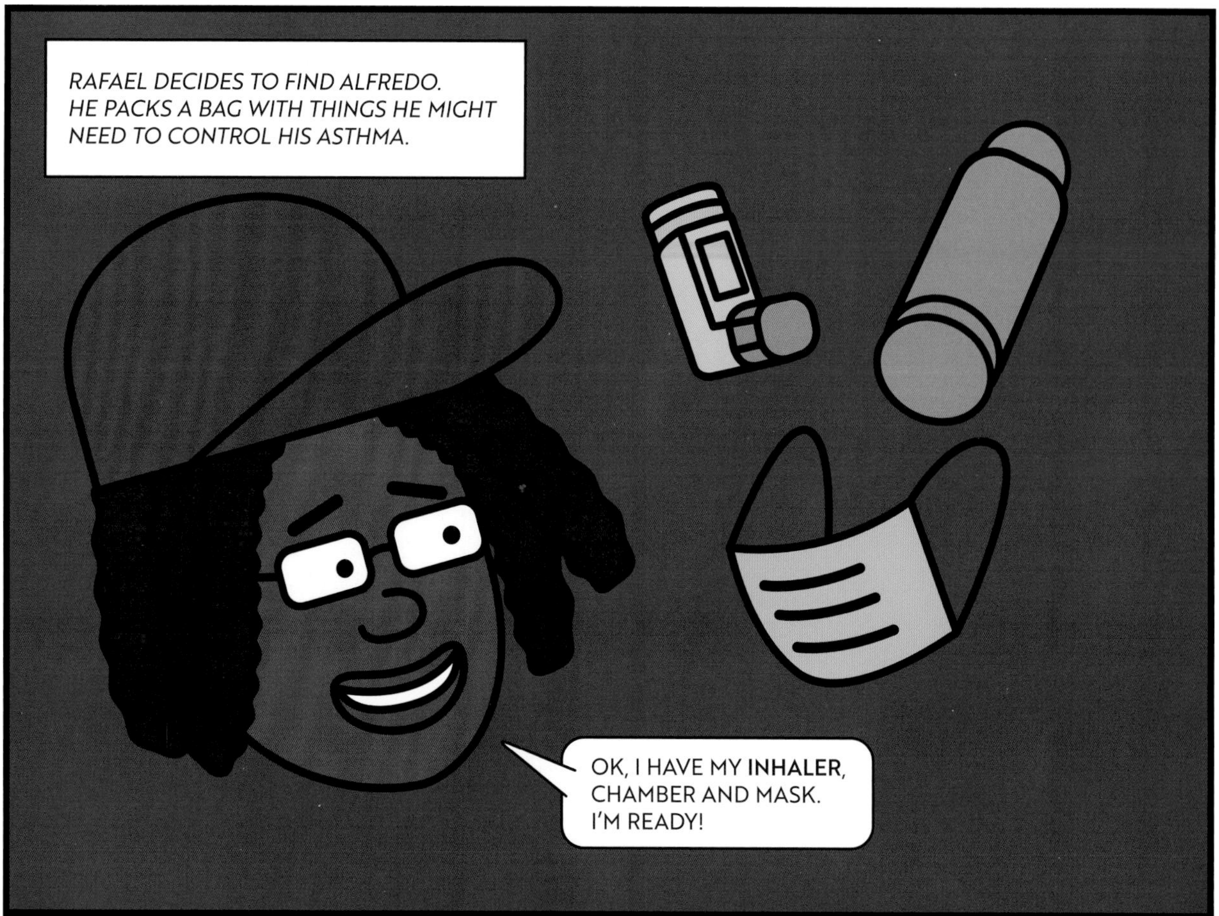
RAFAEL DECIDES TO FIND ALFREDO. HE PACKS A BAG WITH THINGS HE MIGHT NEED TO CONTROL HIS ASTHMA.
OK, I HAVE MY **INHALER**, CHAMBER AND MASK. I'M READY!

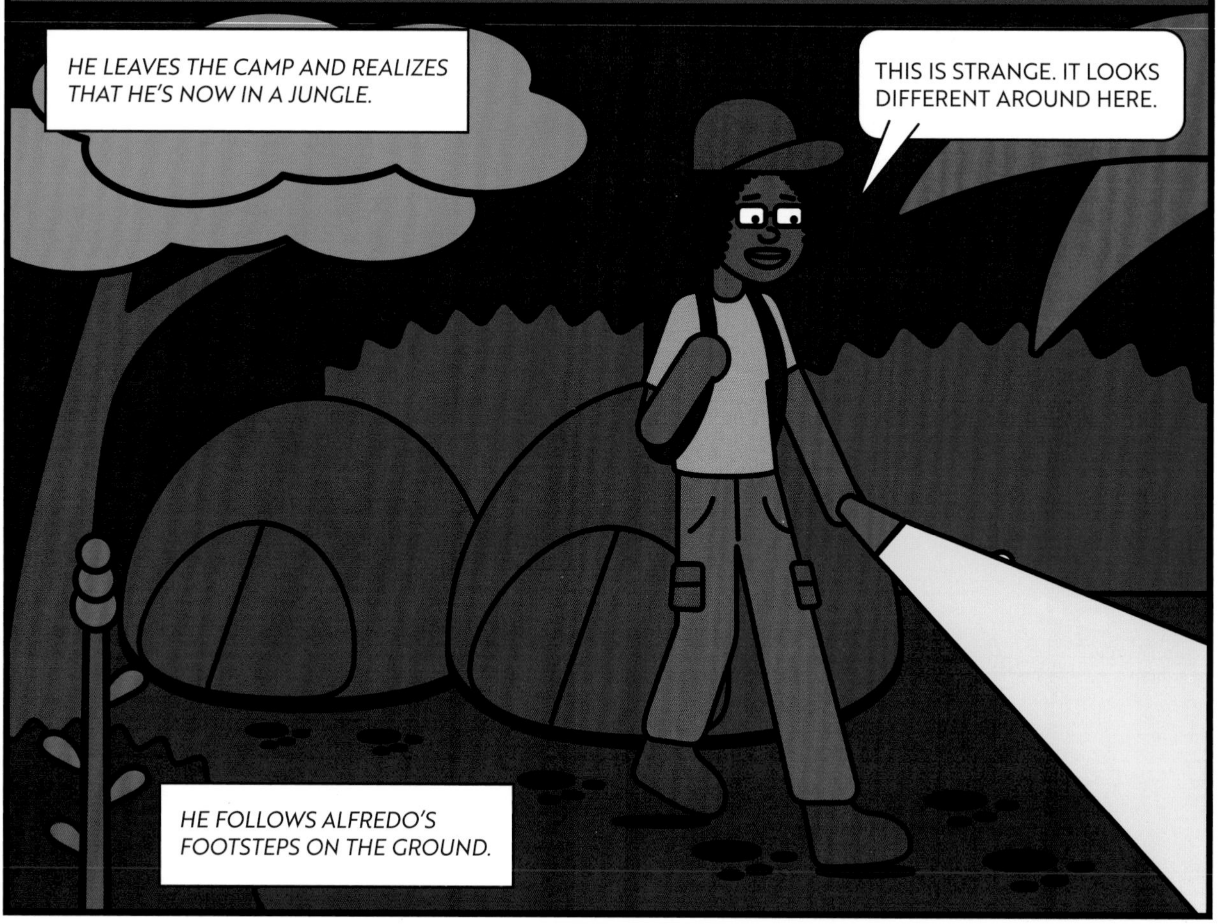
HE LEAVES THE CAMP AND REALIZES THAT HE'S NOW IN A JUNGLE.
THIS IS STRANGE. IT LOOKS DIFFERENT AROUND HERE.
HE FOLLOWS ALFREDO'S FOOTSTEPS ON THE GROUND.

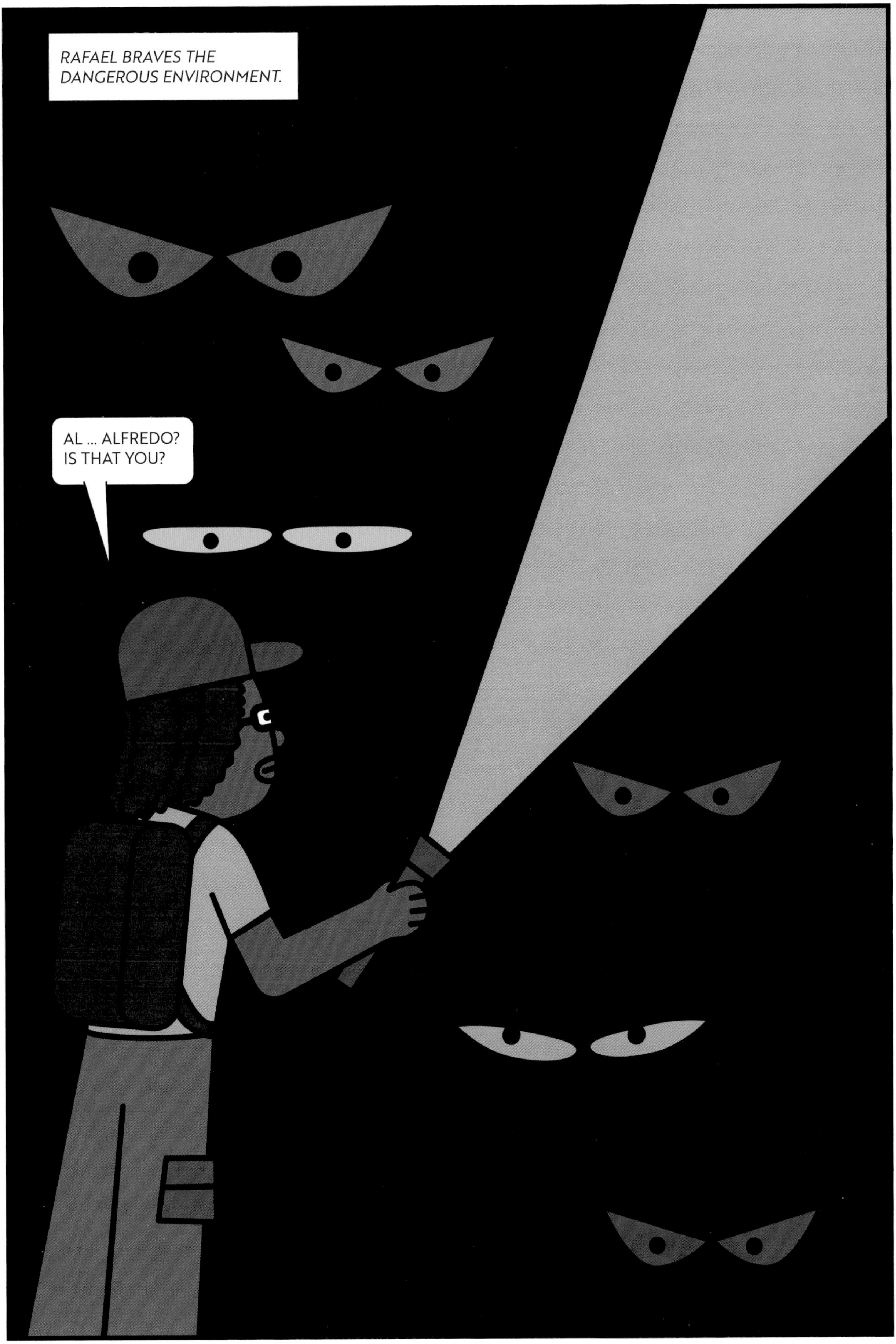
RAFAEL BRAVES THE DANGEROUS ENVIRONMENT.
AL ... ALFREDO? IS THAT YOU?

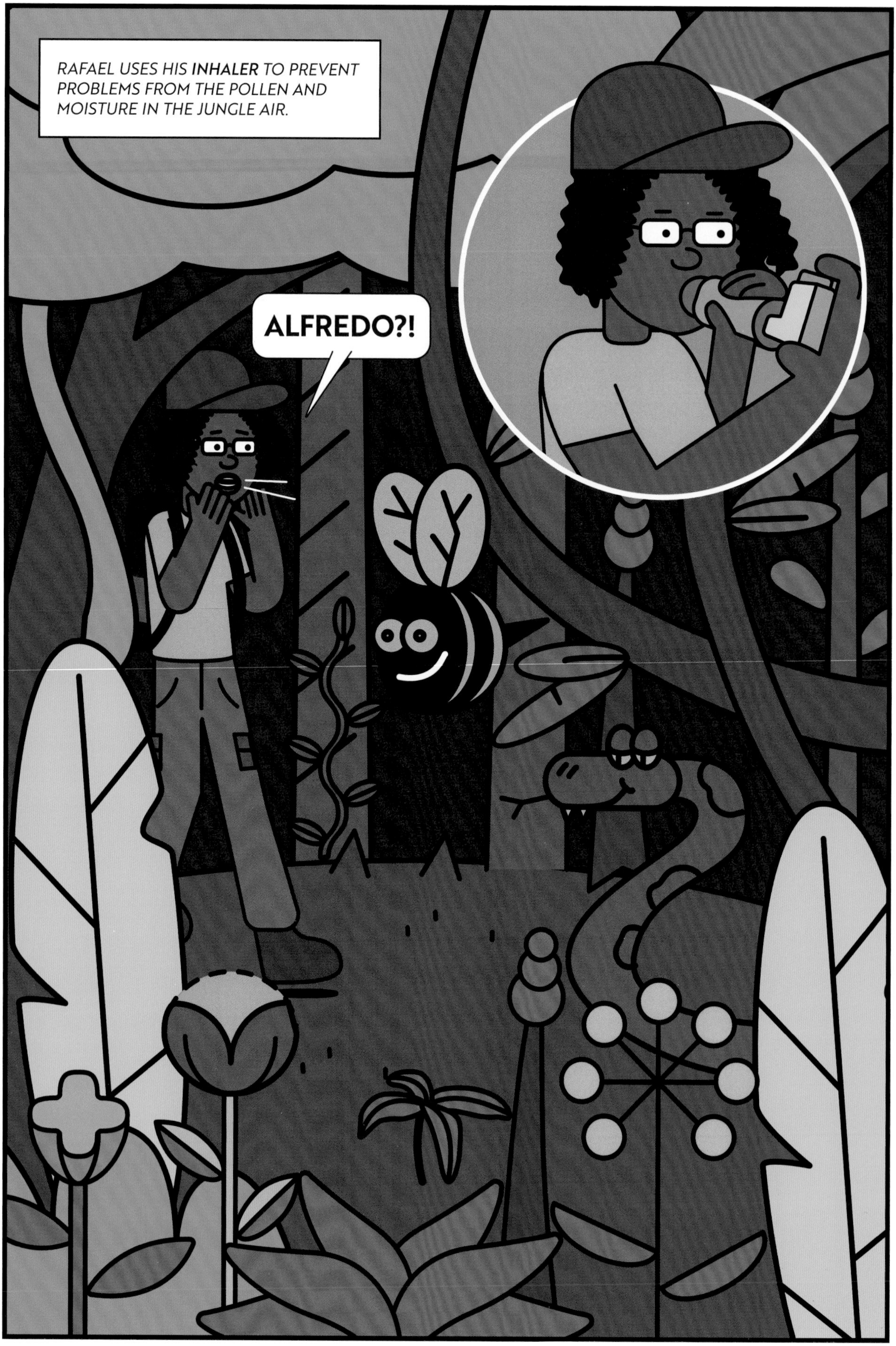

RAFAEL USES HIS INHALER TO PREVENT PROBLEMS FROM THE POLLEN AND MOISTURE IN THE JUNGLE AIR.
ALFREDO?!

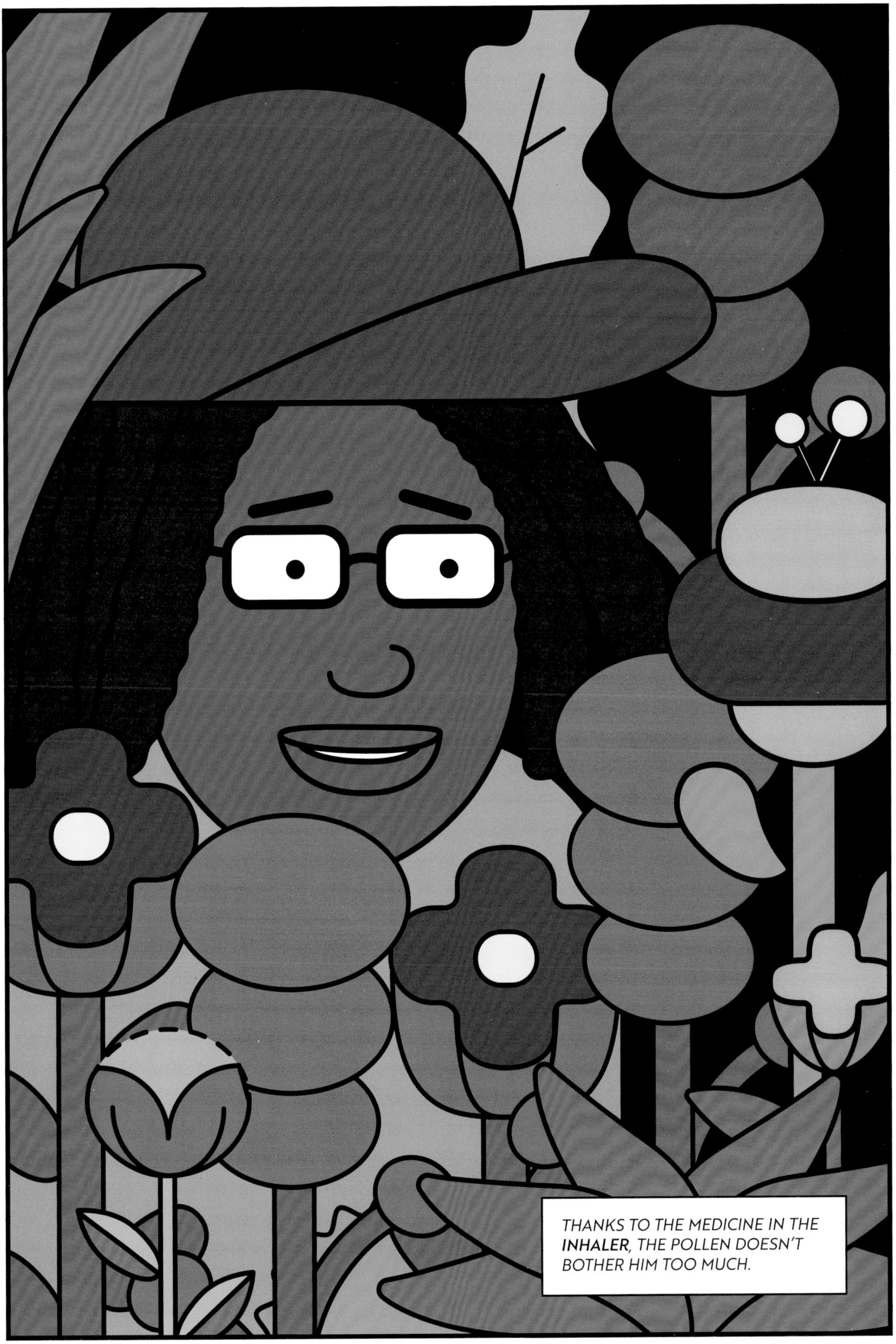
THANKS TO THE MEDICINE IN THE INHALER, THE POLLEN DOESN'T BOTHER HIM TOO MUCH.

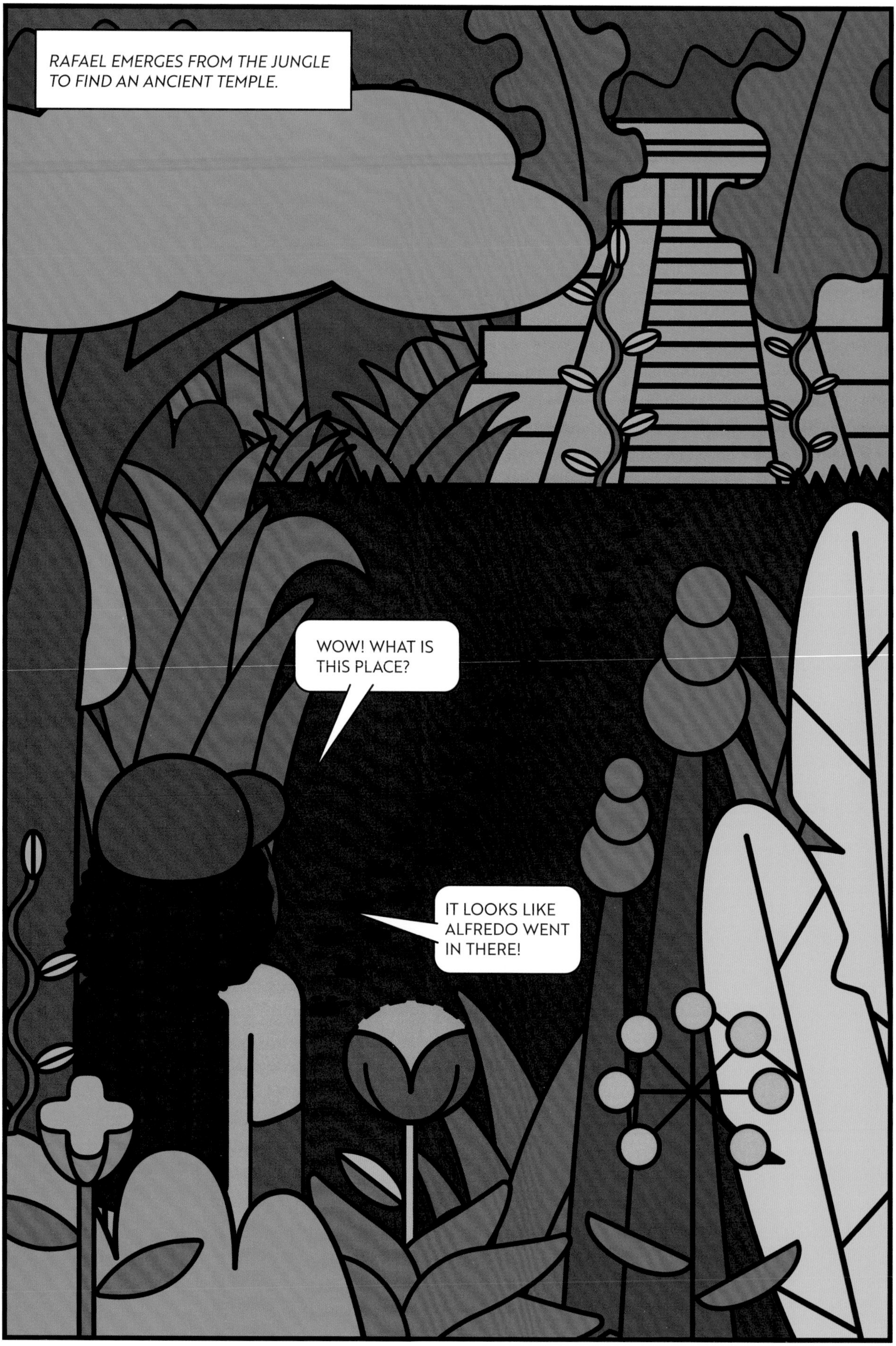
RAFAEL EMERGES FROM THE JUNGLE TO FIND AN ANCIENT TEMPLE.
WOW! WHAT IS THIS PLACE?
IT LOOKS LIKE ALFREDO WENT IN THERE!

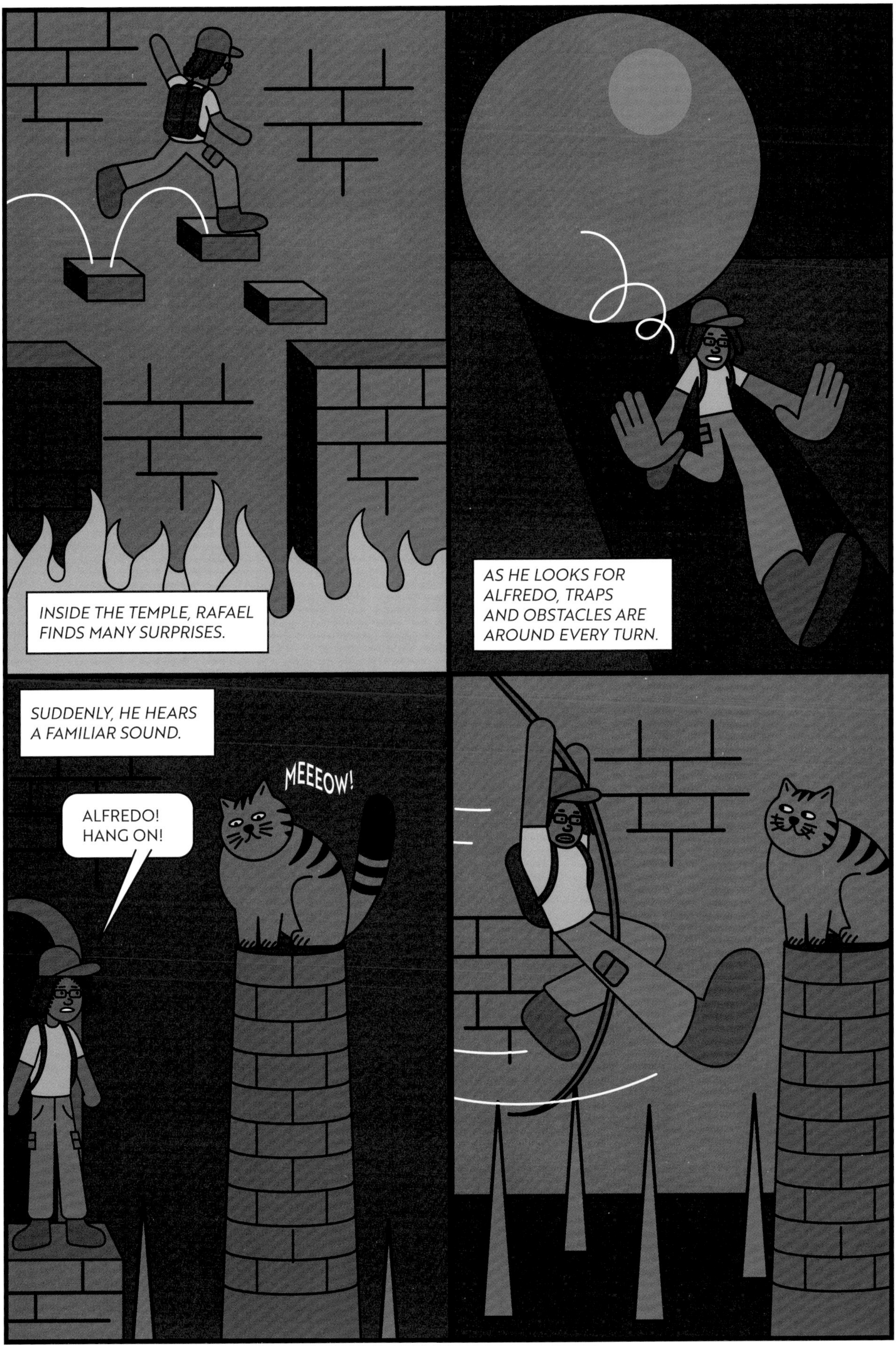
INSIDE THE TEMPLE, RAFAEL FINDS MANY SURPRISES.
AS HE LOOKS FOR ALFREDO, TRAPS AND OBSTACLES ARE AROUND EVERY TURN.
SUDDENLY, HE HEARS A FAMILIAR SOUND.
MEEEOW!
ALFREDO! HANG ON!

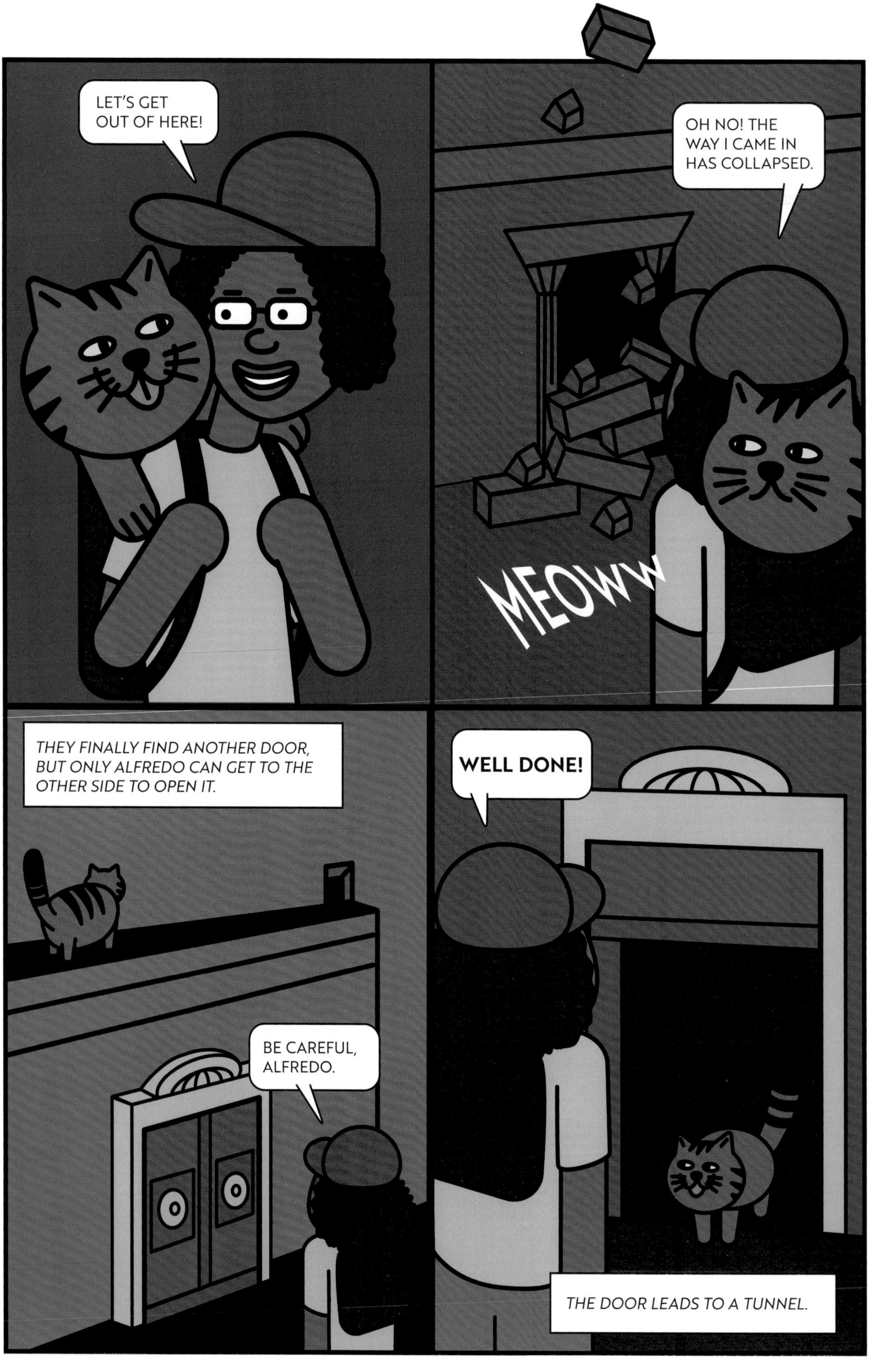
LET'S GET OUT OF HERE!
OH NO! THE WAY I CAME IN HAS COLLAPSED.
MEOWW
THEY FINALLY FIND ANOTHER DOOR, BUT ONLY ALFREDO CAN GET TO THE OTHER SIDE TO OPEN IT.
BE CAREFUL, ALFREDO.
WELL DONE!
THE DOOR LEADS TO A TUNNEL.

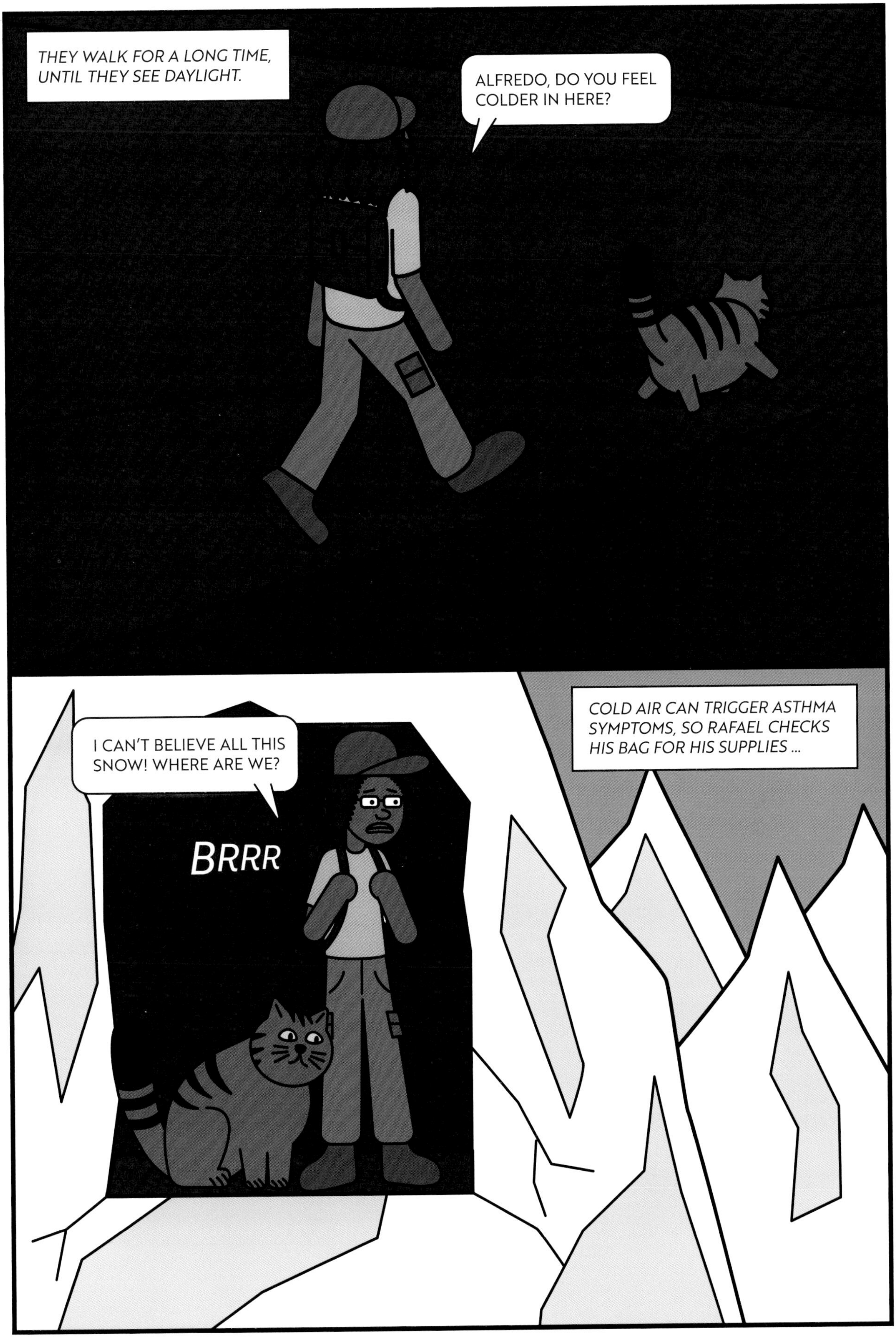
THEY WALK FOR A LONG TIME, UNTIL THEY SEE DAYLIGHT.
ALFREDO, DO YOU FEEL COLDER IN HERE?
I CAN'T BELIEVE ALL THIS SNOW! WHERE ARE WE?
BRRR
COLD AIR CAN TRIGGER ASTHMA SYMPTOMS, SO RAFAEL CHECKS HIS BAG FOR HIS SUPPLIES ...

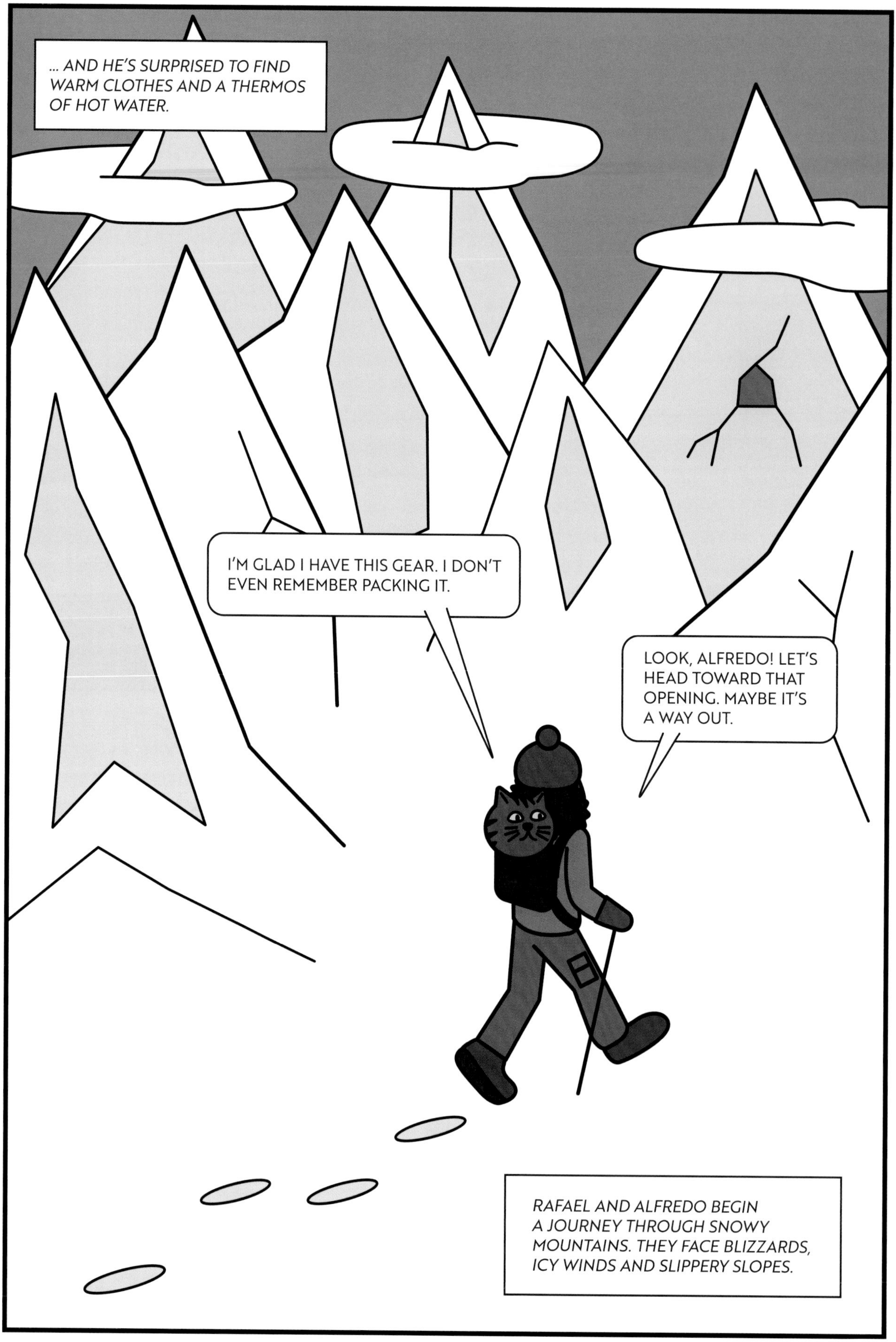
... AND HE'S SURPRISED TO FIND WARM CLOTHES AND A THERMOS OF HOT WATER.
I'M GLAD I HAVE THIS GEAR. I DON'T EVEN REMEMBER PACKING IT.
LOOK, ALFREDO! LET'S HEAD TOWARD THAT OPENING. MAYBE IT'S A WAY OUT.
RAFAEL AND ALFREDO BEGIN A JOURNEY THROUGH SNOWY MOUNTAINS. THEY FACE BLIZZARDS, ICY WINDS AND SLIPPERY SLOPES.

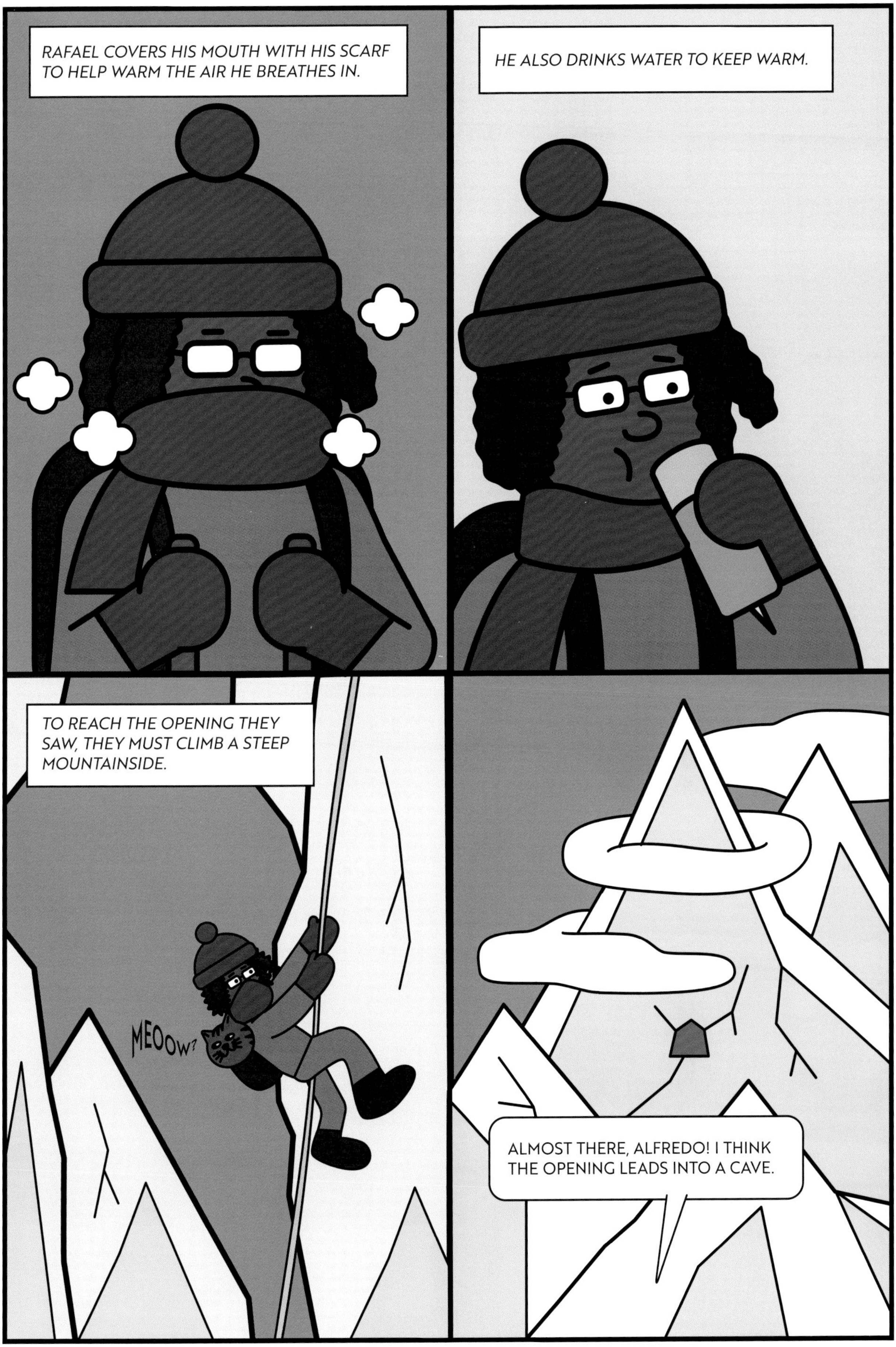
RAFAEL COVERS HIS MOUTH WITH HIS SCARF TO HELP WARM THE AIR HE BREATHES IN.
HE ALSO DRINKS WATER TO KEEP WARM.
TO REACH THE OPENING THEY SAW, THEY MUST CLIMB A STEEP MOUNTAINSIDE.
MEOOW?
ALMOST THERE, ALFREDO! I THINK THE OPENING LEADS INTO A CAVE.

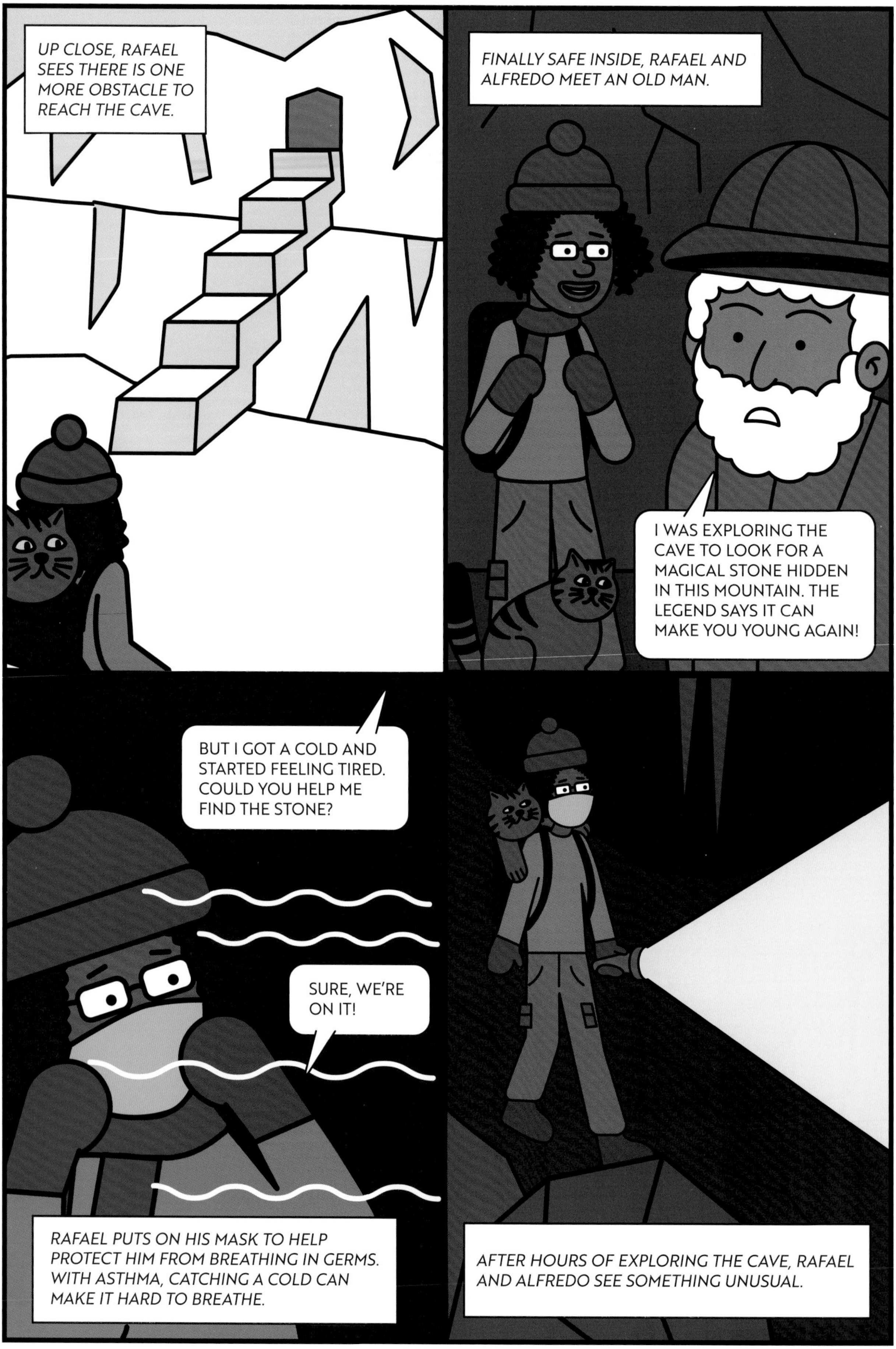
UP CLOSE, RAFAEL SEES THERE IS ONE MORE OBSTACLE TO REACH THE CAVE.
FINALLY SAFE INSIDE, RAFAEL AND ALFREDO MEET AN OLD MAN.
I WAS EXPLORING THE CAVE TO LOOK FOR A MAGICAL STONE HIDDEN IN THIS MOUNTAIN. THE LEGEND SAYS IT CAN MAKE YOU YOUNG AGAIN!
BUT I GOT A COLD AND STARTED FEELING TIRED. COULD YOU HELP ME FIND THE STONE?
SURE, WE'RE ON IT!
RAFAEL PUTS ON HIS MASK TO HELP PROTECT HIM FROM BREATHING IN GERMS. WITH ASTHMA, CATCHING A COLD CAN MAKE IT HARD TO BREATHE.
AFTER HOURS OF EXPLORING THE CAVE, RAFAEL AND ALFREDO SEE SOMETHING UNUSUAL.

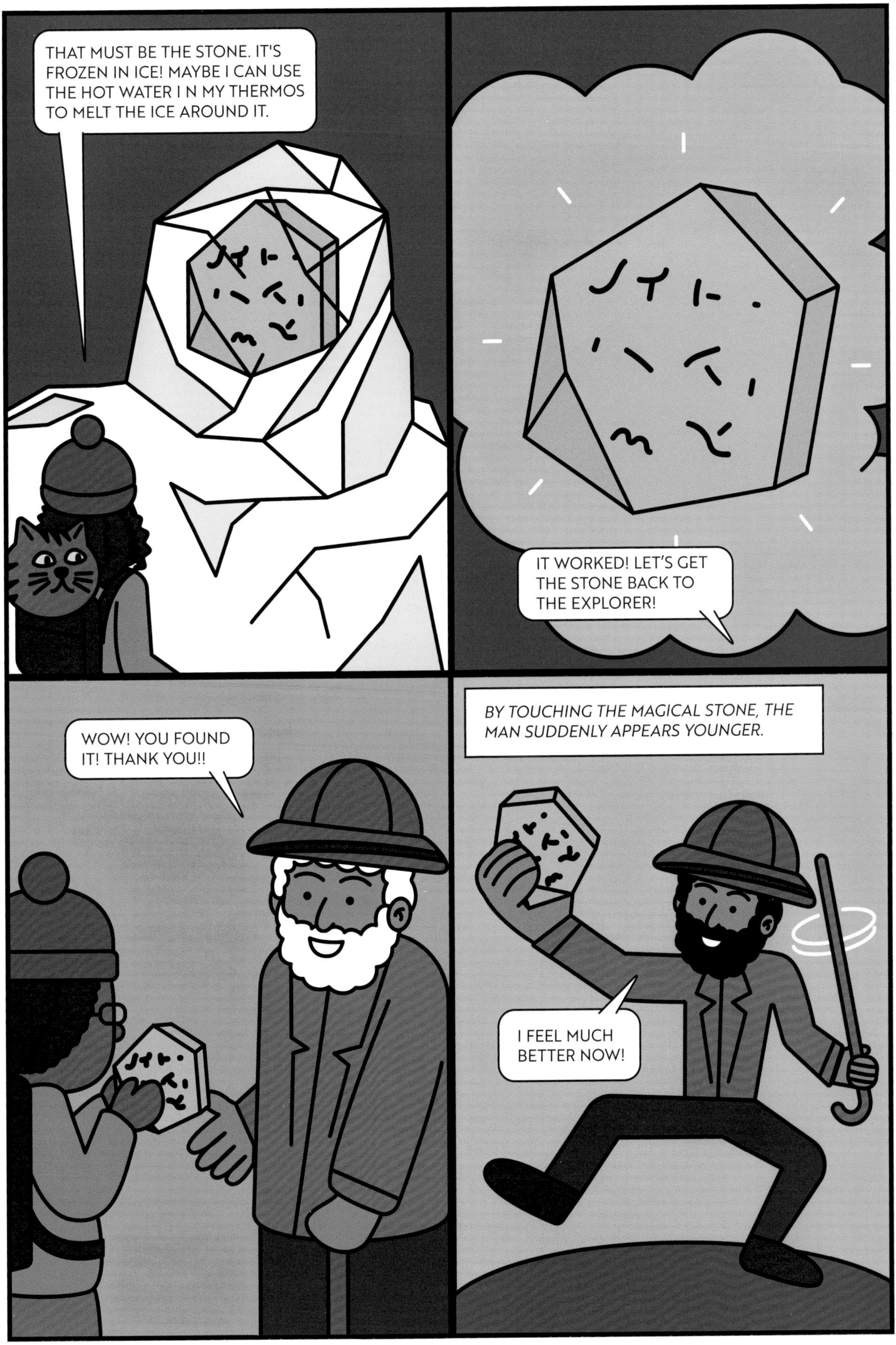
THAT MUST BE THE STONE. IT'S FROZEN IN ICE! MAYBE I CAN USE THE HOT WATER I N MY THERMOS TO MELT THE ICE AROUND IT.
IT WORKED! LET'S GET THE STONE BACK TO THE EXPLORER!
WOW! YOU FOUND IT! THANK YOU!!
BY TOUCHING THE MAGICAL STONE, THE MAN SUDDENLY APPEARS YOUNGER.
I FEEL MUCH BETTER NOW!

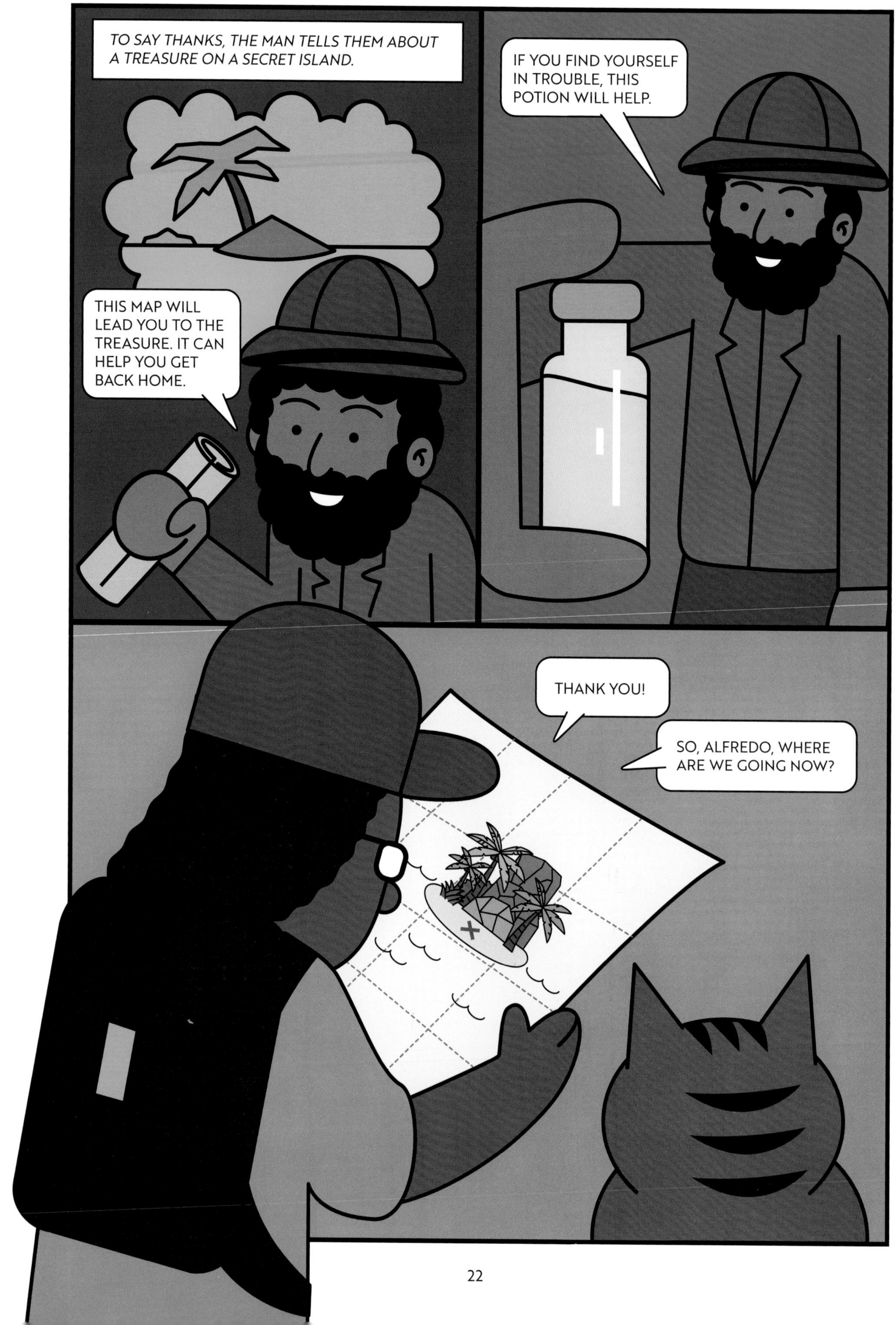
TO SAY THANKS, THE MAN TELLS THEM ABOUT A TREASURE ON A SECRET ISLAND.
THIS MAP WILL LEAD YOU TO THE TREASURE. IT CAN HELP YOU GET BACK HOME.
IF YOU FIND YOURSELF IN TROUBLE, THIS POTION WILL HELP.
THANK YOU!
SO, ALFREDO, WHERE ARE WE GOING NOW?

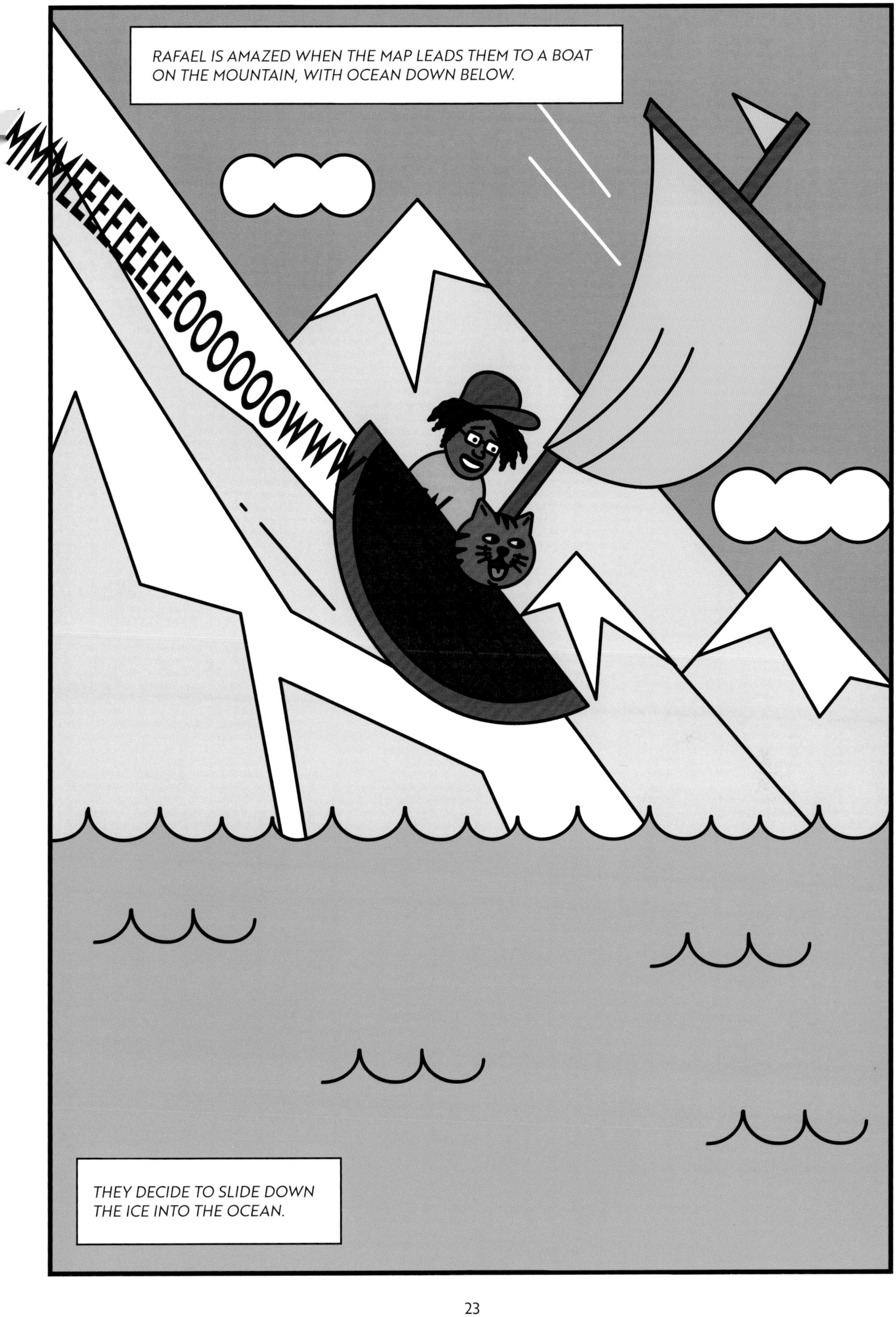
RAFAEL IS AMAZED WHEN THE MAP LEADS THEM TO A BOAT ON THE MOUNTAIN, WITH OCEAN DOWN BELOW.
MMMEEEEEEEEEEOOOOOOOWWW
THEY DECIDE TO SLIDE DOWN THE ICE INTO THE OCEAN.

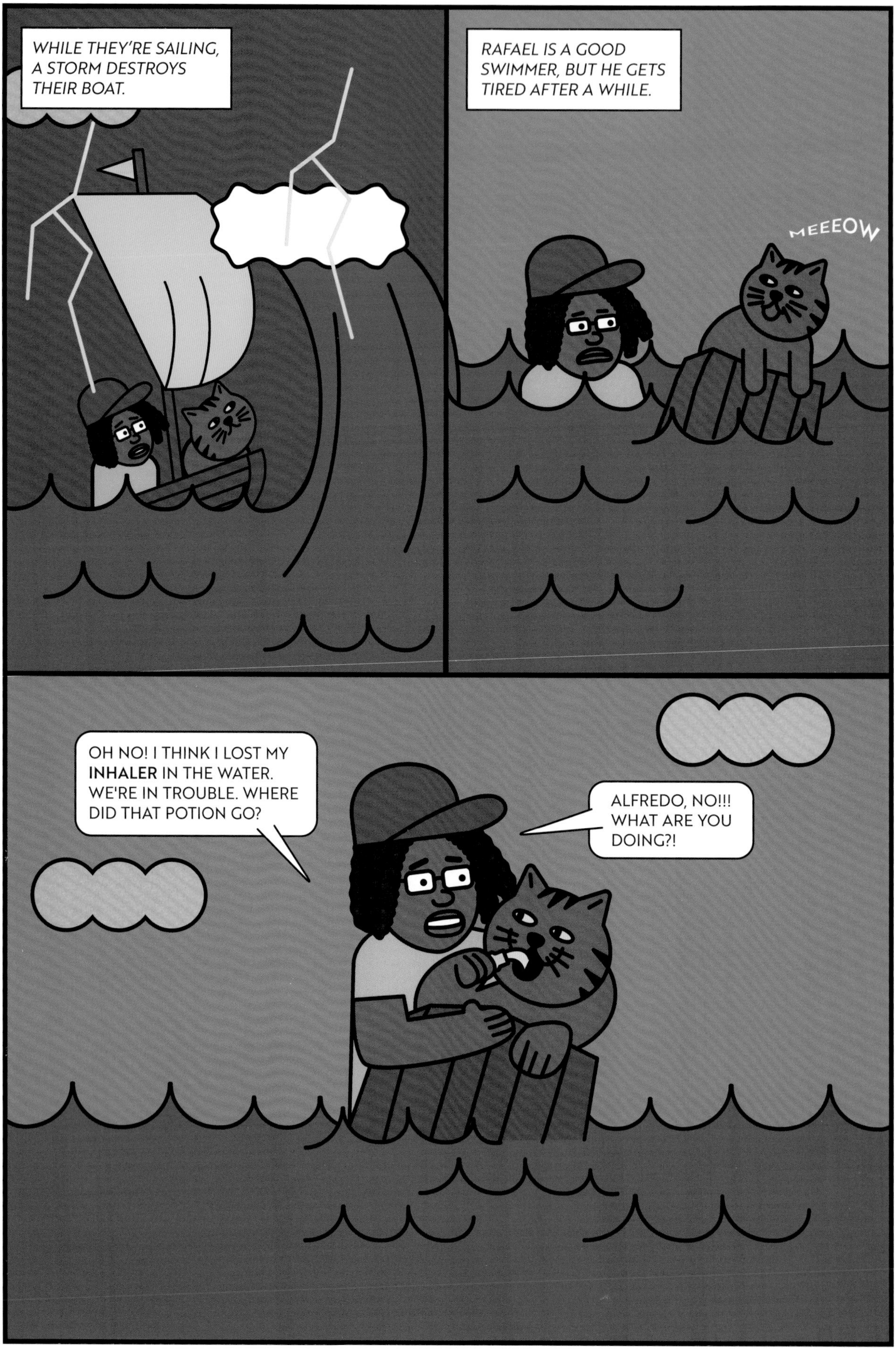
WHILE THEY'RE SAILING, A STORM DESTROYS THEIR BOAT.
RAFAEL IS A GOOD SWIMMER, BUT HE GETS TIRED AFTER A WHILE.
MEEEOW
OH NO! I THINK I LOST MY **INHALER** IN THE WATER. WE'RE IN TROUBLE. WHERE DID THAT POTION GO?
ALFREDO, NO!!! WHAT ARE YOU DOING?!

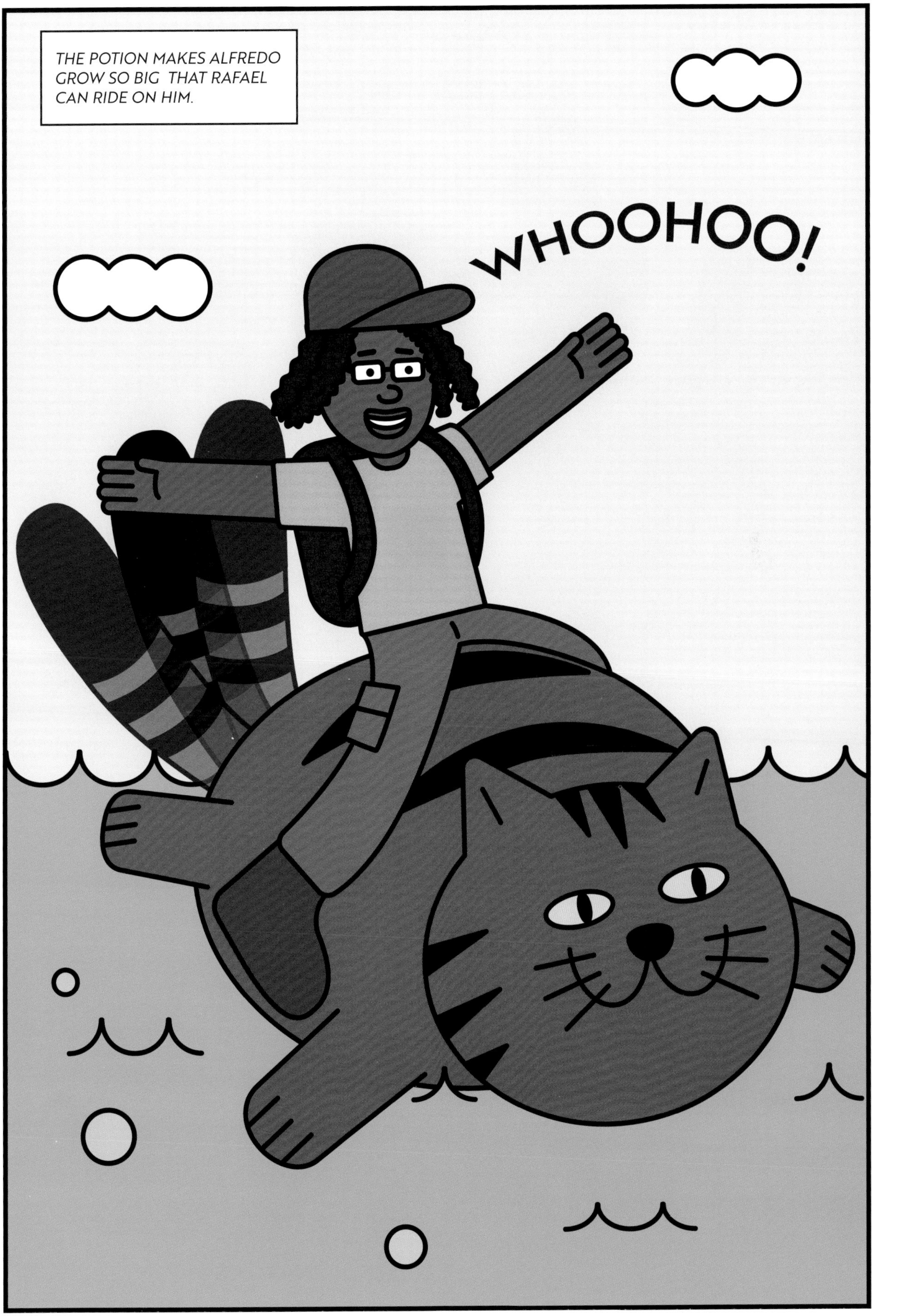
THE POTION MAKES ALFREDO GROW SO BIG THAT RAFAEL CAN RIDE ON HIM.
WHOOHOO!

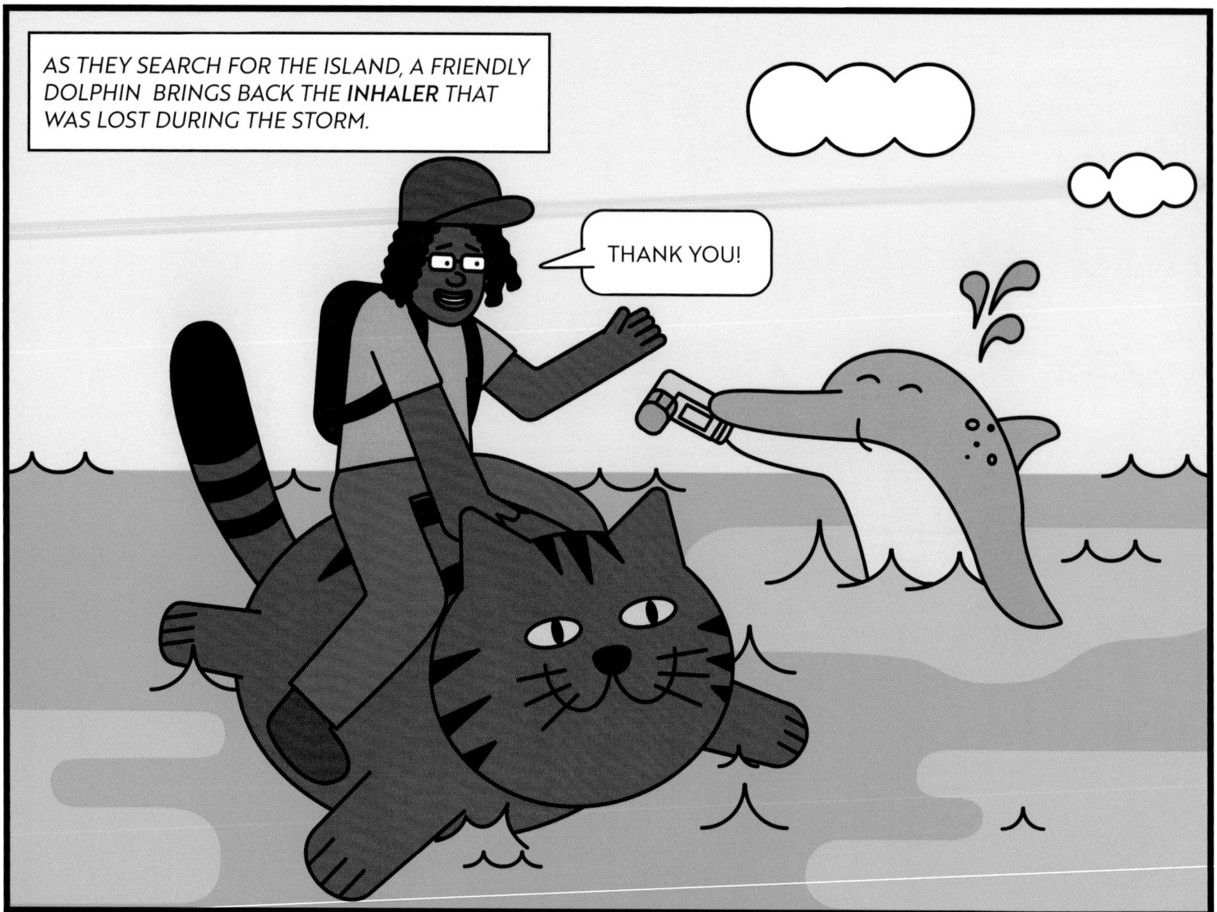
AS THEY SEARCH FOR THE ISLAND, A FRIENDLY DOLPHIN BRINGS BACK THE **INHALER** THAT WAS LOST DURING THE STORM.
THANK YOU!

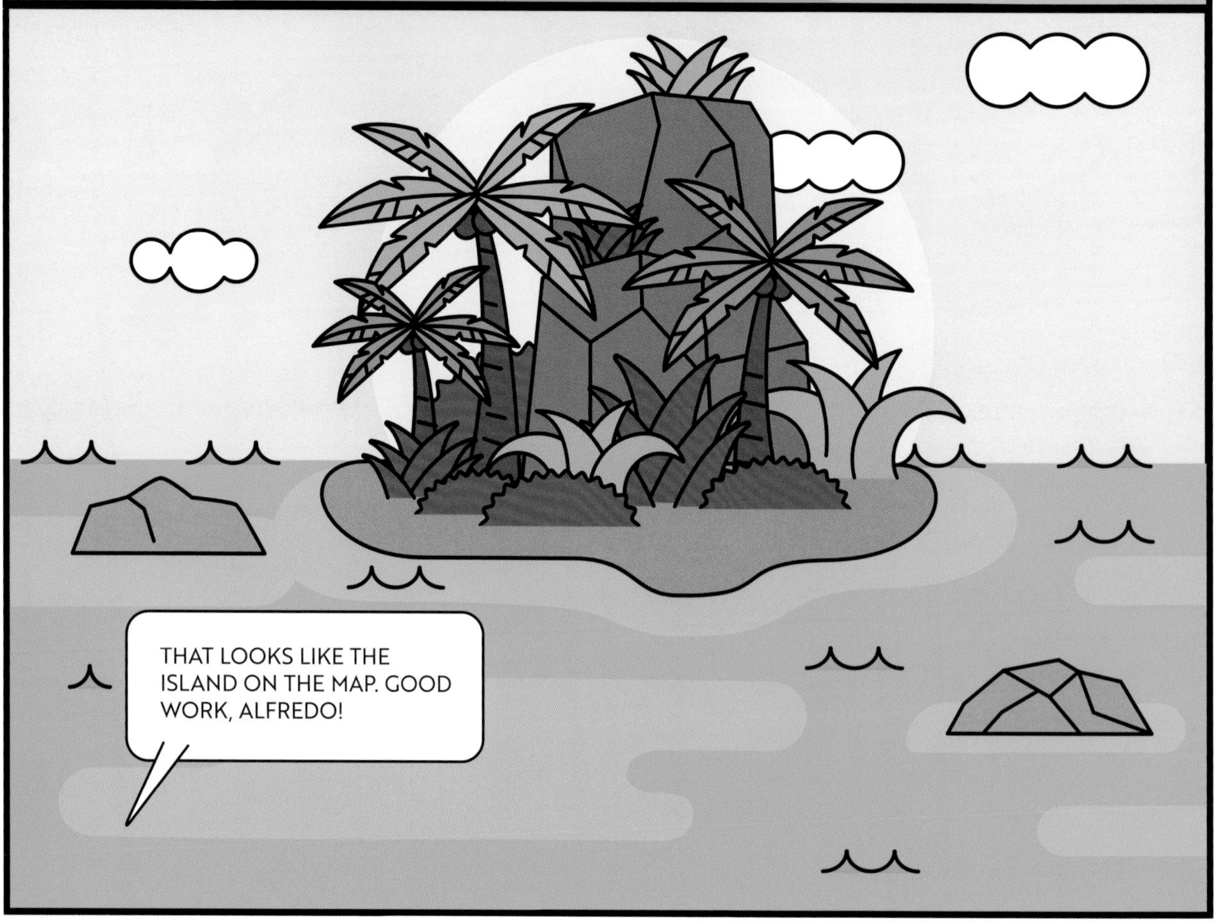
THAT LOOKS LIKE THE ISLAND ON THE MAP. GOOD WORK, ALFREDO!

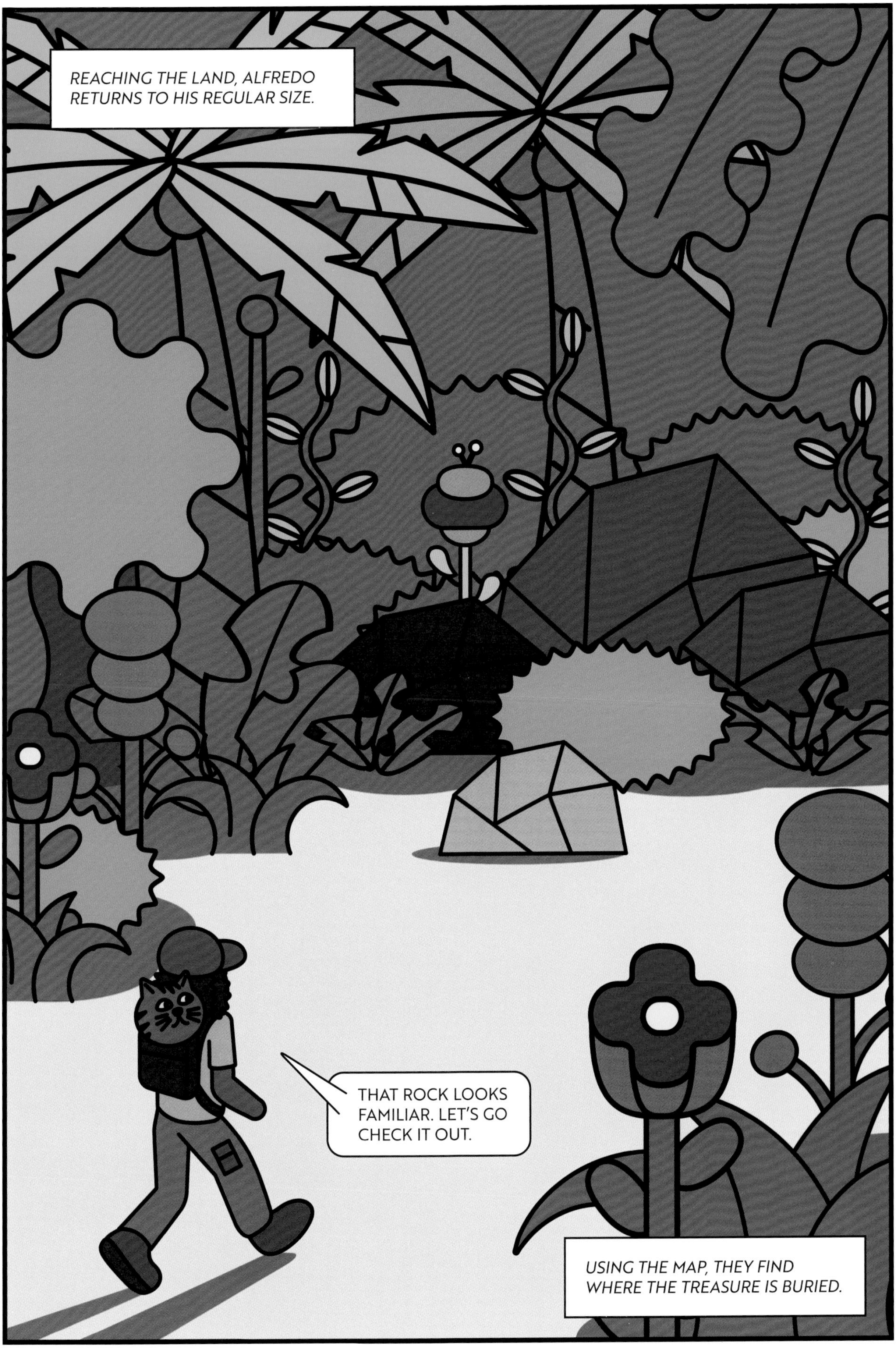
REACHING THE LAND, ALFREDO RETURNS TO HIS REGULAR SIZE.
THAT ROCK LOOKS FAMILIAR. LET'S GO CHECK IT OUT.
USING THE MAP, THEY FIND WHERE THE TREASURE IS BURIED.

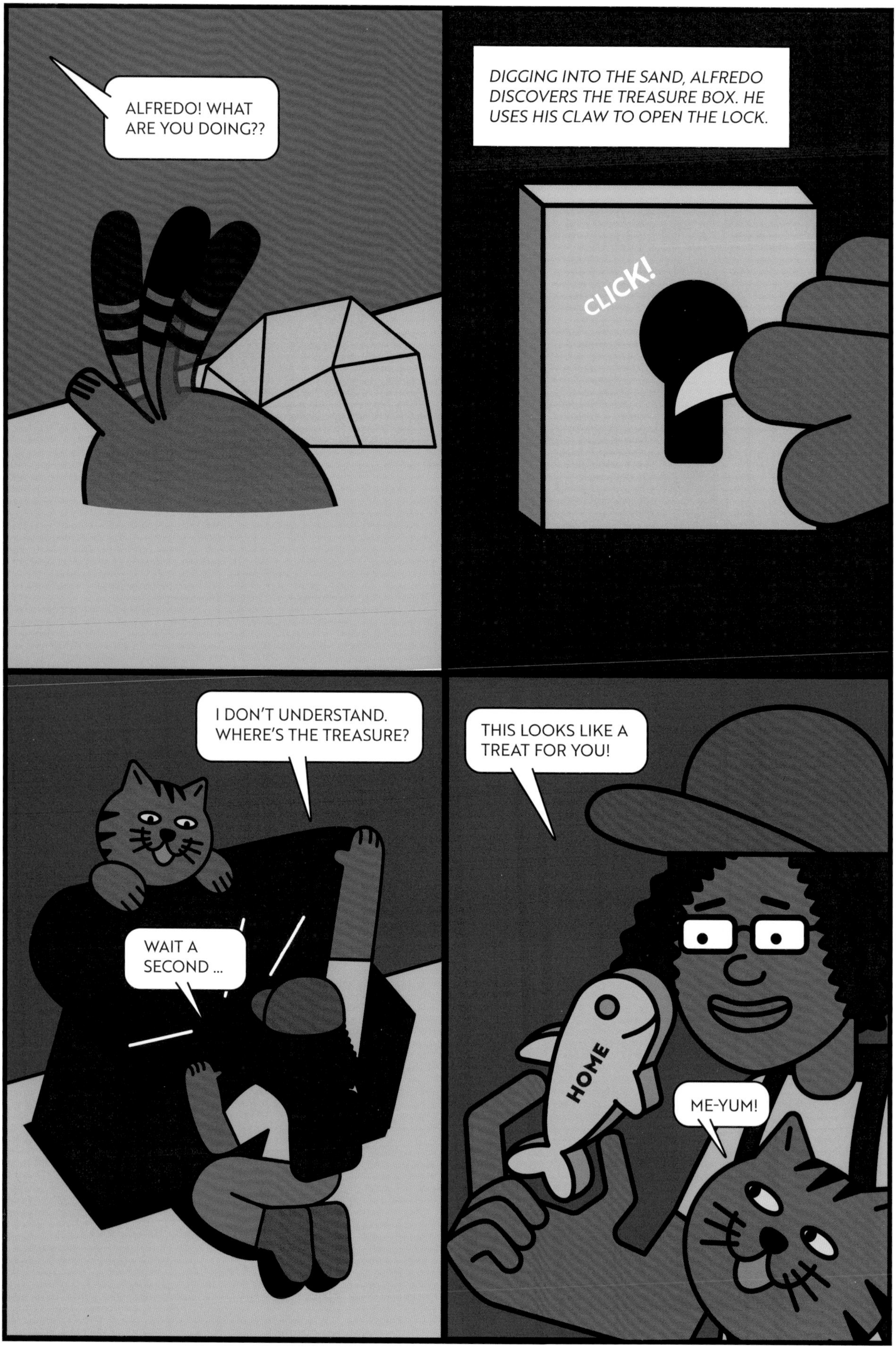
ALFREDO! WHAT ARE YOU DOING??
DIGGING INTO THE SAND, ALFREDO DISCOVERS THE TREASURE BOX. HE USES HIS CLAW TO OPEN THE LOCK.
CLICK!
I DON'T UNDERSTAND. WHERE'S THE TREASURE?
WAIT A SECOND ...
THIS LOOKS LIKE A TREAT FOR YOU!
HOME
ME-YUM!

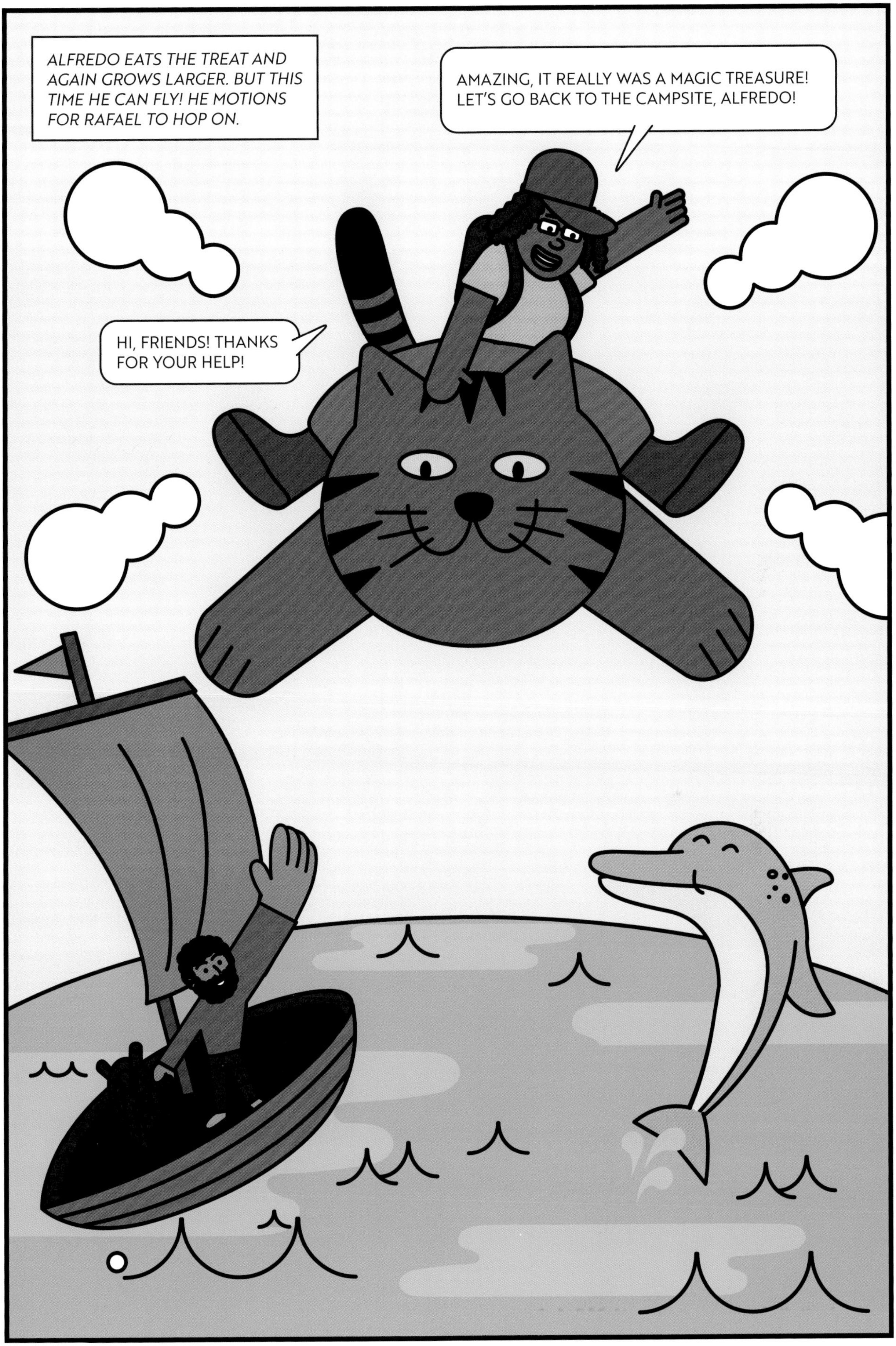
ALFREDO EATS THE TREAT AND AGAIN GROWS LARGER. BUT THIS TIME HE CAN FLY! HE MOTIONS FOR RAFAEL TO HOP ON.
AMAZING, IT REALLY WAS A MAGIC TREASURE! LET'S GO BACK TO THE CAMPSITE, ALFREDO!
HI, FRIENDS! THANKS FOR YOUR HELP!

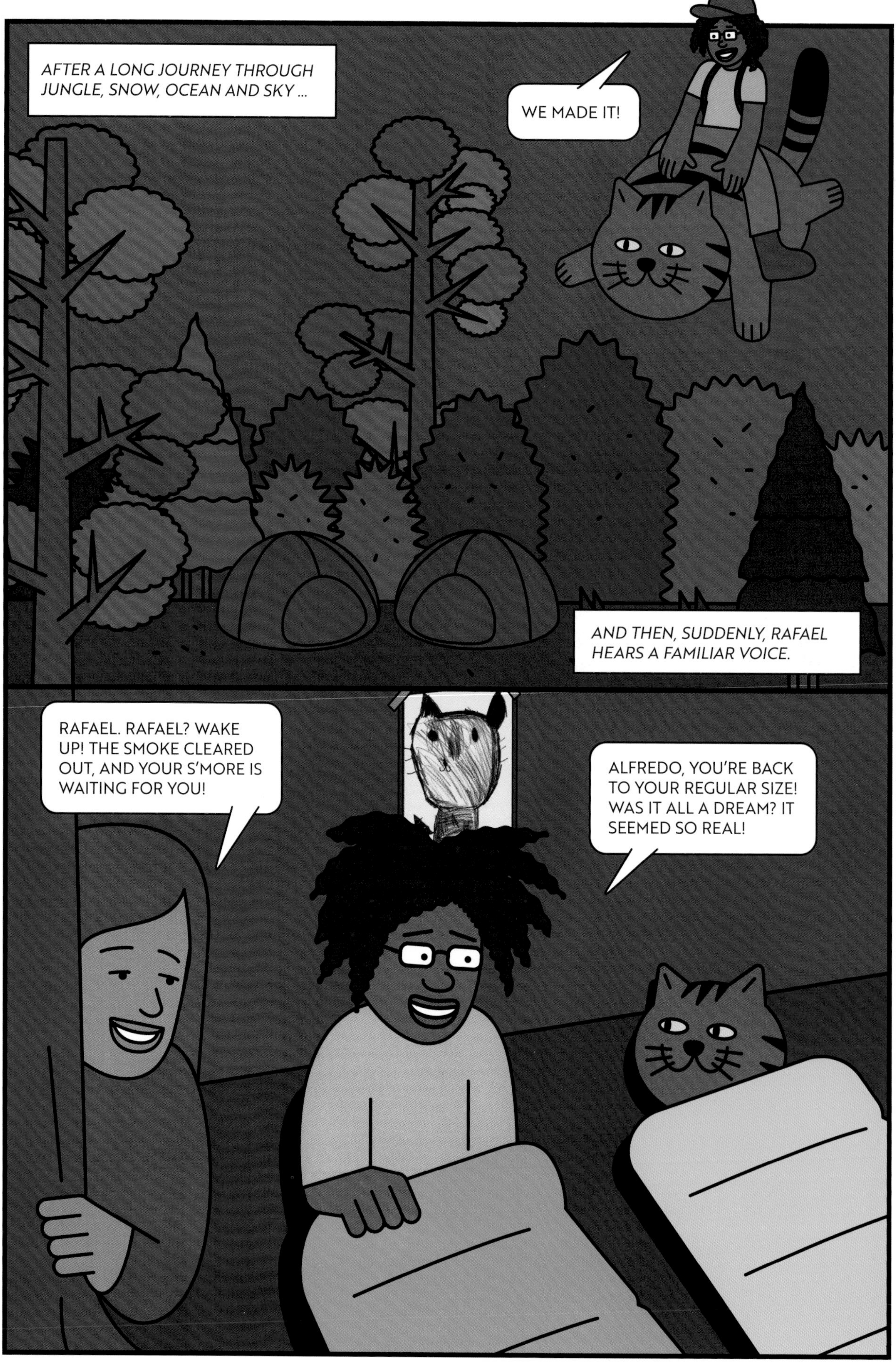
AFTER A LONG JOURNEY THROUGH JUNGLE, SNOW, OCEAN AND SKY ...
WE MADE IT!
AND THEN, SUDDENLY, RAFAEL HEARS A FAMILIAR VOICE.
RAFAEL. RAFAEL? WAKE UP! THE SMOKE CLEARED OUT, AND YOUR S'MORE IS WAITING FOR YOU!
ALFREDO, YOU'RE BACK TO YOUR REGULAR SIZE! WAS IT ALL A DREAM? IT SEEMED SO REAL!

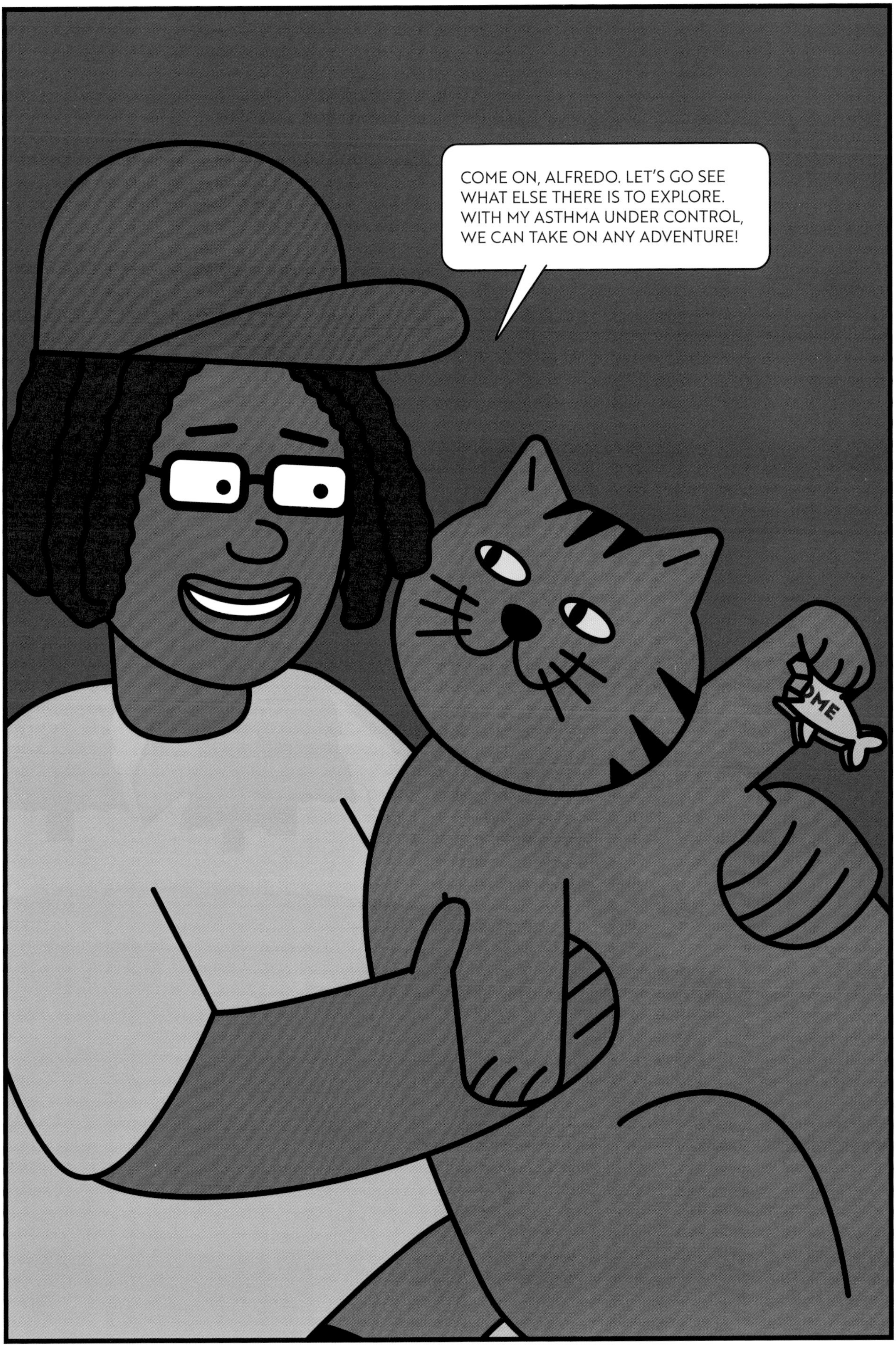
COME ON, ALFREDO. LET'S GO SEE WHAT ELSE THERE IS TO EXPLORE. WITH MY ASTHMA UNDER CONTROL, WE CAN TAKE ON ANY ADVENTURE!
OME

KEY TERMS

acute: sudden or short-term

airways: the tubes that carry air into the lungs when you breathe in

allergic: when you're allergic to something, your body responds to it with an immune reaction that most people don't have. An allergic reaction may include sneezing, itchy skin and trouble breathing.

chronic: long-term

episode: an event that's part of a series or pattern. Asthma symptoms tend to appear in episodes, flaring up and then improving again.

inhaler: a device that delivers liquid medicine in tiny particles that can be breathed in

mouthpiece: part of an inhaler that fits inside the mouth to deliver the medicine

nebulizer: a device that delivers liquid medicine through a mist that can be breathed in

triggers: allergens and other things, such as very cold air, that can cause asthma symptoms

wheezing: breathing with a whistling sound

MORE INFORMATION FROM THE MEDICAL EDITOR

By **Manuel Arteta, M.D.**
Consultant, Division of Pediatric Pulmonology, Mayo Clinic, Rochester, MN; Assistant Professor of Pediatrics, Mayo Clinic College of Medicine and Science

Asthma is the most common long-term (**chronic**) disease in children. Symptoms can start at any age. They often include coughing, difficult breathing and a whistling sound (**wheezing**) when you breathe. These symptoms don't always appear at the same time. But they tend to happen in episodes, which means they get worse sometimes and better again. An asthma attack occurs when symptoms suddenly get worse or become severe. With treatment, the **airway** tightening is reversible, and symptoms get better.

Asthma causes inflammation that narrows the airways — the tubes that carry air into the lungs when you breathe in. Symptoms are caused by inflammation of the small **airways** inside the lungs, called bronchi. To picture inflammation in the **airway**, think about your nose when you get a cold. Your nose swells and fills with snot, called mucus. All that swelling and mucus is from inflammation. With asthma, swelling of the bronchial walls makes the **airways** narrow and fill with mucus. Mucus causes coughing. To make things worse, the inflammation makes the muscles around the bronchial walls twitch. That is when breathing gets harder and **wheezing** gets worse.

Many different things can trigger asthma episodes in different people. Common **triggers** include colds (and other respiratory viruses), exercise, and breathing in things you're **allergic** to, cold air, smoke, or other irritants.

If you have asthma symptoms, visit your doctor's office for a check-up. Asthma might be diagnosed if your symptoms happen in episodes, if they are triggered by common causes, and if asthma medicines help relieve the narrowing in your **airways**. There is no single test for diagnosis. But as part of your visit, you may have a spirometry test, which measures how well air moves in the **airways**.

Treating asthma involves prevention and long-term control. Learning to recognize and avoid your **triggers** is key to preventing symptoms. Medicine also is needed to keep asthma symptoms under control.

Different types of medicines are used to treat asthma. A quick-relief **inhaler** can ease your symptoms right away. This type of **inhaler** delivers bronchodilators, like albuterol, to relax the muscles surrounding the **airways**. When the muscles relax, the **airways** open for easier breathing, but it does not stop the inflammatory process. So symptoms return when the medicine wears off. For long-term relief of symptoms, you need to control inflammation. The best medicines currently available to treat inflammation in asthma and provide long-term control are inhaled steroids.

You shouldn't need to use your quick-relief **inhaler** very often if your long-term control medicines are working properly.

Inhalers deliver medicine directly into the **airways**. The medicine can be given through a machine called a **nebulizer**. Or the medicine can be delivered through a metered-dose **inhaler**, also known as an asthma puffer. The asthma puffer is connected to a holding chamber. An asthma puffer plus a holding chamber is usually preferred because it is easy to take with you, it does not need power and it delivers medicine faster than a **nebulizer**. Also, it has a lower chance of causing side effects, compared with taking pills or a liquid, because the medicine is delivered directly to the **airways** instead of around the whole body.

To keep asthma well controlled, it's important to avoid your personal **triggers** and take anti-inflammatory medicine as often as it is prescribed. Asthma can get worse or better over time. Eventually, most children outgrow it.

REFERENCES

Levy ML, et al. Key recommendations for primary care from the 2022 Global Initiative for Asthma (GINA) update. NPJ Primary Care Respiratory Medicine. 2023. doi: 10.1038/s41533-023-00330-1.

WEB RESOURCES

Just For Kids: Allergy and Asthma Games, Puzzles | AAAAI — www.aaaai.org/Conditions-Treatments/just-for-kids
The American Academy of Allergy, Asthma & Immunology website includes games, puzzles and activities for kids. These are geared to help you learn about managing allergies and asthma in school, on a camping trip and everywhere else you might have your own adventures.

Asthma and Allergies and their Environmental Triggers — kids.niehs.nih.gov/topics/pollution/asthma-and-allergies
Visit this page from the National Institute of Environmental Health Sciences to learn more about how the air around you can affect asthma — both indoors and outside. Then explore games and activities on the website to discover many other ways that the environment is important to your health!

ABOUT THE MEDICAL EDITOR

Manuel Arteta, M.D.
Consultant, Department of Pediatric Pulmonology; Mayo Clinic, Rochester, MN; Assistant Professor of Pediatrics, Mayo Clinic College of Medicine and Science

Dr. Arteta is a pediatric pulmonologist — a lung specialist for children and teenagers — at Mayo Clinic Children's Center in Rochester, Minnesota. In his clinical practice, he is especially focused on severe asthma in children and childhood interstitial lung diseases. He also treats children with cystic fibrosis.

ABOUT THE AUTHORS

Guillaume Federighi, aka **Hey Gee**, is a French and American author and illustrator. He began his career in 1998 in Paris, France. He also spent a few decades exploring the world of street art and graffiti in different European capitals. After moving to New York in 2008, he worked with many companies and brands, developing a reputation in graphic design and illustration for his distinctive style of translating complex ideas into simple and timeless visual stories. He is also the owner and creative director of Hey Gee Studio, a full-service creative agency based in New York City.

Charles was born at 24 weeks of pregnancy, weighing only 1 pound, 11 ounces. Because of his early arrival, his lungs, heart, and brain needed more time to develop. He spent four months in the neonatal intensive care unit (NICU). There, he received care to help him survive and grow. Once he was at home, he remained on oxygen and a monitor for a year. Because of his **chronic** lung disease, he had to get shots for respiratory syncytial virus (RSV), and he has to be careful to avoid too many crowds to prevent him from getting sick. Today, although he is still small, he is a very happy, high-energy 8 year old boy. He attends Spanish immersion school and participates in as many activities as possible trying to keep up with his older brother. He uses his **inhaler** daily and also a **nebulizer** when he gets sick. He lives in Rochester, MN with his family.

ABOUT FONDATION IPSEN BOOKLAB

At the service of the general interest, working toward an equitable society, the Fondation Ipsen BookLab publishes and distributes books free of charge, primarily to schools and associations. Through collaborations between experts, artists, authors and children, our publications, for all ages and in a variety of languages, focus on the education and awareness of issues related to health, disability and rare diseases. Discover our complete catalog online at www.fondation-ipsen.org/book-lab.

ABOUT MAYO CLINIC PRESS

Launched in 2019, Mayo Clinic Press shines a light on the most fascinating stories in medicine and empowers individuals with the knowledge to build healthier, happier lives. From the award-winning *Mayo Clinic Health Letter* to books and media covering the scope of human health and wellness, Mayo Clinic Press publications provide readers with reliable and trusted content by some of the world's leading health care professionals. Proceeds benefit important medical research and education at Mayo Clinic. For more information about Mayo Clinic Press, visit MCPress.MayoClinic.org.

ABOUT THE COLLABORATION

The My Life Beyond series was developed in partnership between Fondation Ipsen's BookLab and Mayo Clinic, which has provided world-class medical education for more than 150 years. This collaboration aims to provide trustworthy, impactful resources for understanding childhood diseases and other problems that can affect children's well-being.

The series offers readers a holistic perspective of children's lives with — and beyond — their medical challenges. In creating these books, young people who have been Mayo Clinic patients worked together with author-illustrator Hey Gee, sharing their personal experiences. The resulting fictionalized stories authentically bring to life the patients' emotions and their inspiring responses to challenging circumstances. In addition, Mayo Clinic physicians contributed the latest medical expertise on each topic so that these stories can best help other patients, families and caregivers understand how children perceive and work through their own challenges.

Text: Hey Gee and Charles
Illustrations: Hey Gee

Managing editor: Anna Cavallo, Health Education and Content Services/Mayo Clinic Press, Mayo Clinic, Rochester, MN
Project manager: Mary E. Curl, Department of Education, Mayo Clinic, Rochester, MN
Manager of publications: Céline Colombier-Maffre, Fondation Ipsen, Paris, France
President: James A. Levine, M.D., Ph.D., Professor, Fondation Ipsen, Paris, France

MAYO CLINIC PRESS KIDS
200 First St. SW
Rochester, MN 55905
mcpress.mayoclinic.org

For bulk sales to employers, member groups and health-related companies, contact Mayo Clinic, 200 First St. SW, Rochester, MN 55905, or send an email to SpecialSalesMayoBooks@mayo.edu.

Proceeds from the sale of every book benefit important medical research and education at Mayo Clinic.

ISBN: 978-1-945564-59-8 (HC); 979-8-887700-65-6 (ePub)

Library of Congress Control Number: 2023947065

Printed in the United States of America